KELSO

Kelso receiving a standing ovation from the overflow crowd after defeating Gun Bow in the 1964 Aqueduct Handicap. (NYRA–Mike Sirico)

KELSO

The Horse of Gold

Linda Kennedy

WESTHOLME
Yardley

Westholme Publishing, LLC
Eight Harvey Avenue
Yardley, Pennsylvania 19067
Visit our Web site at www.westholmepublishing.com

First Edition
First Printing: May 2007
10 9 8 7 6 5 4 3 2 1

ISBN: 978-1-59416-043-1
ISBN 10: 1-59416-043-0

Printed in United States of America

For my parents who encouraged a child to dream.

Contents

The French Camp, at Agincourt:

Dauphin: What a long night is this! I will not change my horse with any that treads on four pasterns. . . . When I bestride him I soar, I am a hawk. He trots the air; the earth sings when he touches it. . . .

Constable: Indeed, my lord, it is a most absolute and excellent horse.

Dauphin: . . . It is a theme as fluent as the seas: turn the sands into eloquent tongues, and my horse is argument for them all. 'Tis a subject for a sovereign to reason on, and for a sovereign's sovereign to ride on; and for the world—familiar to us and unknown—to lay apart their particular functions and wonder at him. . . .

William Shakespeare,
The Life of King Henry the Fifth, III, vii

"He comes into the paddock, with Dick Jenkins, his exercise boy, wearing a crash helmet and a sweater in the gray and yellow colors of Bohemia (Stable).... You see the tense lady who owns him, trying to appear calm, and you note with amusement that once again she has her fingers crossed for luck. You see trainer Carl Hanford, a look of concern on his boyish face.... You see Milo stroll in from the jock's room, debonair in his racing silks, and you know he'll walk up to Mrs. duPont and squeeze her arm solicitously, and always he does just that.

And then you turn to Kelso himself and you shake your head, because you never can quite believe that this is the champion, the greatest there ever was. You'd feel downright sorry for him if you didn't know what he's about to do to all those other horses who are so much prettier than he is.

He's so spare and skinny, at least a hundred pounds under the minimum weight that any race horse ought to scale. He seems awkward and ill at ease.... And then they're in the gate, and the man yells "Go!" and the miracle of motion transforms this homely horse into one of nature's masterpieces."

—David Alexander
The Thoroughbred Record
November 7, 1964

Kelso as a three-year old with Eddie Arcaro up, following his six-length victory in the 1960 Hawthorne Gold Cup. (Hawthorne National)

Introduction

On June 22, 1960, a small brown gelding appeared at Monmouth Park for his first race as a three-year-old, and only the fourth start of his young career. None could know it then, but the ordinary horse that appeared that day would come to dominate American racing like no other thoroughbred before or since. For five unprecedented years, he would reign as Horse of the Year, defeating the best of five generations of thoroughbreds, more than 60,000 foals in all.

I turned twelve that month, and like many girls my age, I idolized horses —particularly racehorses. Early on, I had discovered C. W. Anderson's children's classic, *A Touch of Greatness*, profiles of courageous thoroughbreds from the first half of the twentieth century. By seven, I had my own horse, and by twelve, was living a life rich in fantasy. On summer mornings, I would rise before dawn, sneak out to the pasture, and tack my western pony with an English saddle, jacking up the stirrups to become an "exercise rider." Together, we galloped around our "turf course"—an overgrown five-acre field—sweeping down the straightaway, leaning through the bushes of the first turn, hugging the telephone pole on the far bend, and flying down the stretch, straining toward the "wire" for all we were worth. Sometimes we switched to the dirt track, pounding down the long rural road that led to a neighbor's farm.

I devoured Walter Farley's *Black Stallion* series, and in more serious moments, thoroughbred history as well. I absorbed the achievements of great racehorses, and digested the details of Man o' War's career. I could recite from memory all previous winners of the Kentucky Derby, the year they won, and their winning time. On weekdays, I read the *Herald Tribune*, studying the race charts before school. Come 4:30 P.M. on Saturday, I tuned to New York television's race of the week. On Sunday, the *New York Times* brought results of feature races from all over the country. And once a week, the professional journal, *The Blood-Horse*, arrived. Yet I had never been to a racetrack. The sport of racing existed in the black-and-white shadows of a console television, the still-life of newspapers and magazines, and the poetic prose of the great turf journalists—Joe Hirsch, William Rudy, Mike Casale, Charles Hatton, David Alexander. When Kelso appeared, I was ready—prepared to embrace a legend that had miraculously arrived in my time.

In 1963, the year Kelso was six, just days before the Belmont Stakes and my fifteenth birthday, my father died suddenly, leaving a hole I thought would never fill. That August, in a stroke of love and genius, my mother brought me to Saratoga to see Kelso run in the Whitney Stakes. Hardly a horsewoman herself, it was her idea.

Since 1863, horses at Saratoga had been saddled under ancient elms, each tree bearing the number a horse would carry in the coming race. Skipping the sixth race, I stood alone under tree # 2, waiting patiently, and anxiously, for Kelso to emerge. Gradually, a crowd gathered, but I had secured my place in front.

When he appeared, his dark coat glistening in the sun, I stood motionless, consciously aware I must save this moment forever. If the old elm could only talk! How many admirers had preceded me in the past hundred years, while one champion after another paraded under its arching limbs? Had Man o' War stepped here, forty-three years earlier, as he prepared for the Travers Stakes, and one last duel with Upset and John P. Grier?

Kelso circled in front of me close enough to touch. When the crowd split to allow the champion through, it divided at me. The great brown gelding walked calmly, almost brushing me as he passed, followed closely by Carl Hanford, his trainer. Barely believing my luck, I dared to speak: "He's going to win today, isn't he, Mr. Hanford?" Carl Hanford stopped, placed his hand on my shoulder and looked me squarely in the eye. "I sure hope so," he said with a smile. For Carl Hanford, it must have been one of a million platitudes uttered each time the great horse ran. For me, it was the world.

Kelso won easily that day as I watched from the rail on the finish line, as near as I could be to the sweat, and breath, and pounding hooves. My mother stood beside me, and only now do I realize how much she understood.

There were many young fans like myself, and Kelso's owner, Mrs. Allaire duPont, received mail by the bagful. Ironically, it took years for our adult counterparts to realize what we had known all along. But when they did, it was at once a fever and a love affair. By seven, the "old man" was a heart-stealer. By eight, and nine. . . . When age seemed to slow him down, hearts broke for him, and when it appeared Father Time himself might lose, we pleaded, pounded our fists, exploded in exultation, and sighed with relief.

I t is the destiny of great geldings to race long into maturity, until the achievements of youth are mingled with those of age, and the once young sensation is forgotten in the legend of the "grand old man." Not so the young colt, retired early for a more lucrative career at stud. He is immortalized for a brief string of victories; a short list of memorable deeds, the individual details recorded by history. Thus, we remember Man o' War "breaking John P. Grier's heart," and Secretariat "moving like a tremendous machine," seizing the Triple Crown by thirty-one unbelievable lengths at Belmont. Indeed, the fewer and more mythic the conquests, the greater the legend and more vivid the memories.

Now consider the gelded hero. Gainfully employed only as a professional athlete, he is destined to race until one victorious season blends into the next, and years of championship are merged in a long string of numeric achievements. Picture, for a moment, the great Exterminator. Do you envision an adolescent champion poised in the winner's circle, a blanket of Derby roses draped over young shoulders? Or do you see "Old Bones," the original iron horse, victor of fifty races in a hundred starts? It is as though history would have us believe old geldings were always old, and for longevity alone have achieved the mantle of greatness.

So, let us reexamine the phenomenon that was Kelso. Horse of the Year at three, four, five, six, and seven, and well on his way at eight, it wasn't until his fifth season, at the advanced age of seven, that he attained the public adoration and legendary status awarded lesser colts in other eras.

In his own time, writers would seek to explain the enigma— how a one-in-a-million champion could be overlooked for so long by the general public. Whitney Tower would ascribe lack of early fame to absence from the Triple Crown classics. Others would cite the gelding's spare frame and humble build for failure to stir emotion. David Alexander would assert the need of a fatal flaw to be loved—that it wasn't until time seemed to slow the old warrior down, and victories seemed near-miracles, that the public took the "Old Man" into their hearts. Yet the brilliance of Kelso's youth alone was enough for Eddie Arcaro, rider of Triple Crown champions Whirlaway, Assault, and Citation, to declare him "the best horse I ever rode."[1]

Fortunately, history provides a longer perspective, a sharper lens from which to view the psyche of the times, and human reaction to the events that shaped them. The advent of universal radio lent legendary status to the deeds of War Admiral and Seabiscuit. Newsreels popularized Whirlaway and Citation, enabling non-racegoers to witness faraway feats from hometown theaters. The arrival of black-and-white television brought the "Grey Ghost" of Native Dancer into American living rooms. "Through this electronic medium, he became a regular and welcome guest in the homes of millions who might never thought of visiting a racetrack."[2] In 1960, that same medium launched a charismatic young politician to the Presidency.

When Kelso appeared as a three-year-old in 1960, the Triple Crown races were history, the names of the winners splashed in headlines and embedded in memory. It was Saturday, September 3 before Kelso was seen in a televised feature, and despite an impressive triumph, the small gelding escaped notice.

On October 29, Kelso appeared in our homes again, smashing Nashua's American record for two miles, and laying claim to his first Horse of the Year mantle. Three days later, John Kennedy was elected President. In the three years of Kennedy's term, Kelso achieved three more Horse of the Year titles. On November 22, 1963, two weeks after Kelso laid claim to his fourth consecutive crown, John Kennedy was slain by an assassin's bullet.

When Kelso returned to the races in 1964, the world was a different stage than the one he exited in November. And seemingly for the first time, the public was ready to embrace the champion Kelso had always been. The seven-year-old gelding didn't win that year until June 25, in an unimportant race against a mediocre field. But when the old man regained his form months later, he brought us to our feet and tears in the final hours, surpassing even the finest achievements of his youth. For two wondrous months in the fall of 1964, when Kelso decisively defeated the best horses America and the world could offer, the nation was moved by greatness it had finally come to realize. And it is no surprise the romance of that glorious season lingers in legend, eclipsing the memory of so many youthful accomplishments.

In 1966, at the age of nine, Kelso was retired. That same year, I entered college. The winds of change swept through the nation, and my generation was caught in the fury. Like others, I marched, protested, moved back to the land. I married, raised a child, pursued a career, divorced, saw my child wed, and grandchild born. In the intervening years, I climbed mountains, walked through deserts and canyons, tackled rock faces and frozen waterfalls—all the while seeking a mirror of myself in the elements I embraced. And then suddenly, without forethought, I found myself writing this book, haunted by the straining body of a courageous brown horse who shaped my life in ways I am only beginning to realize.

What follows is the story of Kelso, as seen through the eyes of one fortunate enough to have witnessed the old warrior in his prime. "Courage is that rare coin that returns twofold to the spendthrift, but leaves the miser penniless," wrote C. W. Anderson. I trust Mr. Anderson would have agreed: In Kelso, there was more, far more, than just a touch of greatness.

KELSO

Kelso at age six, winning his third consecutive Woodward Stakes by three and one half lengths with speed to spare. (Bob Coglianese)

Chapter One

Once Upon a Time There Was a Horse Named Kelso . . .

K ELSO'S STORY, LIKE THAT of all thoroughbreds, begins on ancient sands of the Middle East and steppes of Central Asia. There, bred for centuries, rose strains of horses selected for speed, stamina, strength and courage. Among them were three – the Darley Arabian, Godolphin Barb,[1] and Byerley Turk, whose blood would eventually flow in tail-male descent[2] through every thoroughbred living today. But they were not alone. From origins in Arabia, Yemen, Syria, Turkistan, Iraq, Iran, Turkey, and North Africa came almost a hundred others, who by purchase, theft, or the spoils of war inhabited the barns of English nobility in the seventeenth and eighteenth centuries. Bred to swift native ponies and likewise imported mares, their blood too would flow, if not in direct male descent, then through the seed of at least one—male or female—through successive generations, many to modern times. In 1791, Englishman James Weatherby completed eighteen years of research, compiling all known records of pedigree dating back to founding sires and mares. Through Weatherby's "Introduction to the General Stud Book," the new breed of horse, "thoroughbred" for racing, achieved official status. In 1891, the fifth and final edition of the "General Stud Book" was published, listing 102 stallions of Oriental origin, and 90 recorded mares.[3]

By the seventeenth century, racing as a sport of nobility was well rooted in England, with multihorse contests matching the best of private stables over long courses of open landscape. Often they raced in heats, from one mile to four, "repeated until one horse had won twice and proven himself the best of the field."[4] Swift Scottish ponies known as Galloways became the preferred choice of racing enthusiasts,[5] and by late century, breeders were adding Eastern and North African imports to match the increased demands of distance racing. By 1647, the royal racing stable at Newmarket had expanded, with the royal families of Kings James and Charles I frequenting early matches. The English Revolution produced a temporary setback for racing, forcing many of Charles' supporters and Cavaliers to flee England for the shores of a new continent.

It fell to Charles II in 1660 to organize racing. Himself an avid jockey and owner, Charles expanded the royal stable, established Newmarket as the official racing center, and formalized the sport through creation of purses, courses, standards, and rules. "With the prestige of the royal court behind it, racing began to expand, and gentlemen horse owners searched endlessly for the champion that would earn them one of the new "King's Plates."[6]

Three thousand miles west, on the frontier of forested colonies, racing assumed a distinctly American character. European settlers bent their backs to survival, clearing thickly wooded wilderness to raise vegetables, grains, and livestock. "To set aside land for the sole purpose of sport was an intolerable thought. As a result, racing took place on whatever short paths in whatever small areas were available."[7] Soon, colonists were running their horses on narrow settlement streets, in quarter-mile dashes favoring quick breaks and early speed to secure the best "piece of track."

By the late seventeenth century, new opportunities appeared, and racing followed. In 1658, a vast treeless expanse was discovered on Long Island—"sixteen miles long by four miles broad . . . where you shall find neither stick nor stone to hinder the horse-heels or endanger them in their races."[8] In 1665, a year after the Dutch surrendered New Amsterdam, the English Governor of New York ordered construction of the first formal course on the new continent—two miles round, with silver cups "to be run for each spring and fall."[9] "Blessed with this natural advantage, the leadership in organized racing was more or less thrust upon New York."[10]

In the South, too, geography intervened. Southern tobacco proved an intensive crop, depleting soil nutrients, and rendering fields useless for further planting. By 1690, tobacco fields lay fallow, "some still furrowed," and race fields emerged on their surface, "foreshadow[ing] what was to become the standard American race course, a ellipse or circle approximately 1 mile in circumference."[11] The tradition of British gentry rerooted, and distance racing exploded, with southern tracks hosting "grueling match races similar to those in England and New York."[12]

In 1730, the first English thoroughbred, a twenty-one-year-old son of the Darley Arabian and Byerley Turk Mare, arrived in the New World. "From that point on, Americans set about creating their own version of the thoroughbred, blending imported horses with their own native Indian ponies"[13] and mares of "country stock."[14] Scorned as "mongrel-bred"[15] by some, it came as a shock to New York breeders in 1763 when purebred Old England, the son of an imported mare, was distanced[16] by Maryland "mongrel" True Briton.[17] To this day, at the root of early American distaff lines, including those of Kelso and Man o' War, can be found native mares of unknown origin.

When the British Stamp Act strained relations with England, rebellious colonists passed the first Non Importation Act, suspending import of thoroughbreds from England. "Any war may be expected to cause more or less of an upheaval . . . but the Revolutionary War, particularly as it affected racing and breeding, was virtually a demolition job."[18] Much of America's best breeding stock fell on the battlefield. Others, "through theft, abandonment, or flight"[19] kept their lives but lost their identity, rendering useless most pedigree records to date. By war's end in Virginia, "running through the stud books which survived is the pathetically monotonous entry, 'last record.'"[20]

The import of English horses resumed with fervor. In 1798, Diomed, a direct male descendant of the Byerley Turk—and first winner of the Epsom Derby—was imported to America at the advanced age of twenty-one. A failure at stud in Europe, Diomed encountered immediate success in the early states, producing so many offspring he is remembered today as "the father of American thoroughbreds."

War again intervened, and for two decades surrounding 1812, virtually no imports arrived, leaving the American strain once more independent. During that time, British racing altered form, replacing long matches of multiple heats with single dashes between younger horses. In America, Union Racecourse opened in 1821 on Long Island, sporting the first "skinned" surface, considerably faster than grass strips, and "the model for future American tracks."[21]

Disdainful of the British shift, distance racing in America continued with passion. In 1823, Union hosted the first regional contest between North and South, pitting American Eclipse against the south's Sir Henry in a contest of four-mile heats. Cruelly flogged and bleeding, Eclipse survived twelve miles to seize immortality, prevailing in two of three brutal heats. These great rivalries lasted until 1845, and though they "attracted more crowds than any other event in American history to that point, the real match-up between North and South, in the Civil War, brought racing to its knees."[22]

By 1865, racing in the Atlantic states of the Confederacy had been destroyed, and those areas least scarred by war, most notably

Kentucky and New York, survived to become historic hubs. But the legacy of dirt roads and fallow fields continued to resonate on the bare surface of American tracks, the unique national ground on which precedent demanded achievement.

Nearly a century later, in 1956, Maryland breeder Mrs. Richard C. duPont sifted British bloodlines, seeking the right stallion for her American-bred young mare Maid of Flight. "One part science, two parts faith,"[23] she later recalled the union. Her faith was in Your Host, a California colt of English blood, whose courage had triumphed on track and off. Her science was that of "out-crossing"—the merger of the best British blood with the best developed on American soil.[24]

Allaire duPont was a Renaissance woman, an accomplished equestrian, pilot, mother, and widow of aviation pioneer Richard C. duPont. Born Helena Allaire Crozer of Philadelphia's Main Line, her relationship with horses began with a small pony received from her grandfather. As a youth she competed in horse shows and foxhunts, and as a young adult became Master of Foxhounds at a local Maryland club. In 1934, she married Richard C. duPont of Delaware's illustrious duPont family. They were, by all depiction, a dashing and adventurous young couple.

In 1932, Richard flew the length of the Amazon River in an open-cockpit plane, and by 1934, was breaking soaring records, establishing a sailplane distance record of 158 miles and an American altitude record of 6,223 feet. Soon, Allaire was gliding to records of her own: a woman's altitude record of 5,000 feet, and a solo endurance record of 5 hours, 31 minutes from Pennsylvania to North Carolina in a DuPont glider. An old family photo depicts her crashed in the Everglades, "calmly sitting on the wing of the plane, waiting for Richard to . . . pick her up."[25] Despite her daring deeds, Allaire duPont remained shy, soft-spoken, gentle, and gracious. "Class—sheer class," they would say of her in racing circles, not the class born to wealth, but the real class of character worn on her sleeve.

In 1939, the young couple purchased a cattle farm on the Maryland banks of the Bohemia River. It was "virgin country then, perfect for Allaire's foxhunting,"[26] and the duPonts used it for raising Black Angus of their own. By 1943, Richard was at war, leading an aerial night reconnaissance for the invasion of Sicily. Decorated for his daring mission, he perished soon after, testing one of the Army's newest gliders. His young widow never remarried, devoting her energy to their two young children and lifelong love of horses.

By 1950, Allaire duPont had established a small thoroughbred operation with a few broodmares, and a handful of runners, racing in the name and silks of Bohemia Stable. In 1953, she purchased a well-bred two-year-old filly, unplaced in her first two starts. The filly, Maid of Flight, proved better than average, running third in the Margate and Jeanne d'Arc Stakes at two, and returning at four to finish second in the Philadelphia Turf Handicap. By the spring of 1956, she was ready to be bred, and through her flowed half the science of Mrs. duPont's equation.

American breeders have long recognized the unique power of the dam to forward traits of her father, maintaining broodmare sire records to quantify the progeny of daughters. Indeed, historian Charles Hatton asserts: "Bedouins always have placed . . . the emphasis on the maternal line."[27] In 2006, genetic research began to validate these observations, linking mitochondrial DNA with two key components of stamina: the biochemical systems of energy release and muscular respiration.[28] Through Maid of Flight spiraled the genes of her father, Count Fleet, and her mother's father, Man o' War. And in them were contained two of the pinnacle achievements of American blood.

Man o' War was a legend, a tail-male descendant of the Godolphin Barb, and the standard by which all others—past, present, and future—would be measured. "In the sixteen months between June 1919 and October 1920, [he] rewrote the record books,"[29] winning twenty of twenty-one stakes—from five furlongs* to a mile-and-five-eighths—running on straight courses and ovals, clockwise and counter-clockwise,[30] often carrying 130 pounds or more.[31] He seized the Belmont Stakes by twenty lengths and the Lawrence Realization by a hundred. His effect was electrifying. Following victory in the Belmont Stakes, the *New York Times* recorded:

> The race left no doubt in the minds of all turfmen present that they had seen the greatest horse of this or any other age. . . . It is safe to say Man o' War is a superhorse for the ages as far as records go back; a horse the likes of which will probably never be seen by the present generation of horsemen. . . . The son of Fair Play has set a mark which all horses save himself are likely to shoot at vainly for many years to come.[32]

As a three-year-old, "Big Red" had no equal—shattering three world records, two American records, two track records, and equaling one more—at seven distances from one mile to a mile-and-five-eighths. Years later, turfwriter/historian Joe Palmer would observe: "He did not beat, he merely annihilated. He did not run to world records, he galloped to them."[33]

Count Fleet, too, could "make a clock run backwards."[34] A son of Hall of Fame champion Reigh Count, young Fleet proved a men-

---

*A furlong is one-eighth of a mile. The word derives from a "furrow long," the length of one furrow in a plowed field. A horse running a quarter mile (two furlongs) in 24 seconds is racing at 37.5 miles per hour.

ace in his first two starts, swerving at the break and bumping his rivals. Convinced he was unsafe, owner John D. Hertz placed him for sale. Rider John Longden begged otherwise: "When that leggy brown colt wants to run, he can just about fly," Longden implored.[35] "The colt's dangerous," Hertz insisted. "Someday I'm afraid he'll do you injury." "I'm not afraid," Longden replied,[36] and Count Fleet stayed, seizing three of his next five starts, including the Wakefield Stakes. After an astonishing six-furlong work in 1:08 1/5—a full second faster than the American record—Count Fleet dropped his next race, and never lost again.

The Champagne Stakes fell to Count Fleet in 1:34 4/5, breaking the track record for a mile, and the world record for a two-year-old. The Pimlico Futurity dropped next—by five lengths, equaling the track record for a mile-and-a-sixteenth. The Walden followed suit—this time by thirty lengths—with Fleet eased at the wire. "The gaunt ghost of a horse,"[37] weighing 978 pounds, had seized ten of fifteen starts, was never worse than third, and ended the year as 1942 Two-Year-Old Champion. Assistant trainer Charles Hewitt described: "They fault his conformation, but he can do the job. . . . He doesn't pound the ground like most horses. He doesn't have to dig in and push, but sort of rocks along as if it were the easiest thing in the world."[38]

By three, Count Fleet had grown to a handsome thousand pounds. He was small, but like a "skyrocket flaring across the sky," the brown colt made 1943 "Count Fleet's Year."[39] He rattled off an allowance race at Jamaica Park despite nicking a foot, and won the Wood Memorial so impressively that Arthur Daly of the *New York Times* suggested, "It is a lead-pipe certainty now that the parallel between Count Fleet and Man o' War is going to be more sharply drawn."[40]

The Kentucky Derby proved a three-length cakewalk "without [Count Fleet] even getting up a full head of steam."[41] Once again, he nicked a foot in the running. The Preakness fell by eight lengths, with Fleet eased at the wire. "The Withers. . . . was nothing more than a workout,"[42] as the brown comet streaked home tailing six lengths of open daylight.

Only two outclassed rivals appeared for the seventy-fifth running of the Belmont Stakes. It was Count Fleet by eight lengths at the half, twelve at the mile, twenty as he turned for home, and it was Count Fleet by twenty-five lengths at the wire, "galloping through the stretch run"[43] in the fastest Belmont Stakes to date.

Once again, the overreaching colt had rapped an ankle, and this time it proved his ruin. Rider John Longden later explained: "'I felt him bobble in the stretch and knew he had hurt himself.' . . . 'I started to pull him up, but he'd have none of it. He just grabbed the bit in that bull headed way of his and took off again.'"[44]

Despite plans to bring him back, the injury resisted treatment. His flame too soon extinguished, Count Fleet was retired, sixth winner of the Triple Crown and 1943 Horse of the Year. In 1950, the young stallion was bred to Man o' War's daughter, Maidoduntreath, and the resulting foal was Maid of Flight.

Maid of Flight's illustrious parentage was a significant factor in Allaire duPont's union, but it was Your Host who inspired the breeder's faith. In the injured frame of the young stallion flowed the English blood of eighteen tail-male descendants of the Darley Arabian, a nearly unbroken string of gifted runners and sires. Often small at birth and late to mature, they were stamped with uncommon speed and endurance, excelling at long routes, and passing those traits to multiple generations.

In 1877, it was Kelso's great ancestor Hampton. At five, the small colt matured, "stamp[ing] himself as a weight carrier and stayer of exceptional merit,"[45] securing eight of ten major distance events, including the Kelso Gold Cup[46] under the enormous burden of 139 pounds. Hampton passed this exceptional strength to offspring, a "characteristic [that] persisted in many of his descendants for generations."[47]

Two generations later came Hampton's grandson Bayardo, "one of the greatest horses ever to grace the English turf."[48] Brilliant from six furlongs to two and a half miles, Bayardo seized twenty-two of twenty-four races, including the two-plus-mile Ascot Gold Cup, and the mile and three-quarter St. Leger Stakes, longest leg of the British Triple Crown. Possessing an odd quirk recalled a century later, the brown colt "frequently liked to stand still and look off into the distance for long periods of time, even doing so before some of his races."[49]

Bayardo died young, leaving only seventy-one foals, but two Triple Crown winners, including 1918 champion Gainsborough. Willing, intelligent, and strong like his father, Gainsborough added the two-plus-mile Newmarket Gold Cup before retiring. Considered a great source of stamina at stud, he led the British sire list for two years, culminating with Your Host's grandfather, Hyperion.

Described as "weakly" in early accounts, young Hyperion was so small he required a special feed bin adapted to his size. "There was also some thought given to having the little fellow gelded, sold as a cull, or even destroyed."[50] Hyperion was spared, and though the colt remained small—achieving only 15 1/2 hands[51] at maturity—trainer George Lambton was so "impressed with his beautiful action and by his head so full of courage and character"[52] that he took a chance, and a year later, that faith was confirmed. At two, Hyperion was promising, sprinting five furlongs at Ascot in course record time, dueling to a dead heat at six furlongs, and completing the season with victory in the prestigious Dewhurst Stakes.

At three, he proved his mettle, seizing the two longest legs of the British Triple Crown—the 153rd Derby in race-record time, and the St. Leger Stakes in a three-length romp. With Lambton's health failing, the two parted ways, but Hyperion returned at four, securing his first two races under 138 and 136 pounds. The Ascot Gold Cup proved beyond the colt's tether, but his pre-race performance spoke more of character than victory might have: "In the parade ring prior to the Gold Cup, Hyperion spotted Lambton, wheelchair bound, and in a remarkable display of affection, stopped dead in front of his former trainer, refusing to move on for some time."[53]

In the breeding shed, Hyperion was a stunning success, one of the top three English sires for eleven years between 1939 and 1955. At the height of his career, American film mogul Louis B. Mayer offered Lord Derby a blank check for Britain's invaluable stud. Derby's defiant response: "Even though England be reduced to ashes, Hyperion shall never leave these shores." He never did, producing 118 stakes winners from 524 foals, including eight winners of thirteen classics on both sides of the Atlantic. Mayer imported Hyperion's son, Alibhai, for the highest sum yet paid for an untried yearling. Unraced due to injury, Alibhai ranked with the ten best American stallions for eleven years, producing fifty-four stakes winners, including Your Host, the subject of Mrs. duPont's faith.

Born small and runty, with mismatched eyes and ears set an inch lower on one side than the other, Your Host was a colt plagued by misfortune. As a weanling, he suffered a spinal injury, resulting in a twisted vertebra, crooked neck, and oddly lateral stride. At two, he contracted a near-fatal illness. But the proud youth bounced back. Racing with his "twisted neck low, and his head . . . tilted to the side,"[54] he seized the Del Mar Futurity and California Breeders Champion Stakes before the season ended. "It's what you can't see that matters," trainer Sunny Jim Fitzsimmons once said of champions, and more than one writer applied his words to the gallant chestnut.

Dubbed "Sidewinder" and "Twister" by fans—the "magnificent cripple" and "California Comet"[55] by the press—Your Host returned at three better than ever, reeling off the mile-and-a-sixteenth San Felipe Stakes, and California's launch for Kentucky hopefuls, the mile-and-an-eighth Santa Anita Derby. Come spring he was en route to Churchill Downs, streaking east in a railcar boasting, "Kentucky bound, Derby winner 1950."[56] However brazen, owner William Goetz had reason for confidence. His awkward colt was crackling fast, and if blood didn't lie, would savor the extra furlong of the Derby.

At Keeneland, Your Host "blistered"[57] the track, shattering the course record for seven furlongs, leaving winners of the Blue Grass and Flamingo Stakes six and a half lengths in his dust. Eastern skeptics climbed on board, and "The Sidewinder"[58] was installed Kentucky Derby favorite—with the biggest question of all still hanging: "The railbirds and the hardboots are baffled in seeking comparisons. Is he like Olympia and Coaltown, or is he like Count Fleet and Johnstown? All were incredibly swift. But the first two faded in the later stages of the Derby and the latter two zoomed all the way to greatness."[59]

True to form, Your Host scorched the opening quarters at Churchill Downs.[60] On the backstretch, Mr. Trouble drove past on the rail: "There were cries of 'Your Host is through!' But he wasn't through—not yet. . . . Your Host went back to the head end, and led 'em into the stretch as the thrills began to pile one on top of the other. Longden said later that 'I thought I had plenty of horse left.'"[61]

He didn't. One by one, eight horses drove past, leaving Longden and Your Host to stagger home ninth in the second fastest Derby run to date. Returned to California, Your Host never again ran so poorly, becoming "a terror at medium distances the rest of the season,"[62] reeling off victories in the Kent, Dick Welles, Sheridan, and

Golden State Breeders Handicap. He dropped the Premier Handicap by a nose, was shipped to Chicago, ran third in the Arlington Classic, and, tackling a mile and a quarter for the second time, ran third to Horse of the Year Hill Prince in the American Derby. In November, revenge was sweet as the Sidewinder bounced back to defeat Hill Prince and Ponder by a head and a nose in the mile-and-a-sixteenth Thanksgiving Day Handicap.

On January 1, Your Host appeared for his four-year-old debut in the San Carlos Handicap. Conceding five pounds to Bolero at seven furlongs, he ran second to the latter's new world mark. Five days later he returned, shouldering 130 pounds in the mile-and-an-eighth Santa Catalina Handicap. With seven furlongs down and two remaining, the colt's saddle slipped forward, leaving rider Eric Guerin clutching his mane to stay seated. In a stunning display, Your Host kept Guerin balanced, "weaving his way across the track,"[63] and winging to victory in record-breaking time. It is how the classy colt deserved to be remembered. And but for his next start, and Maid of Flight's foal, he might well have been.

On January 13, the stalwart colt was back for the San Pasqual Handicap, his third start since the New Year. Turning for home, he surged for the lead. In front, Renown lugged in. It was over in an instant. Your Host clipped Renown's heels, "pitched forward and slammed to the dirt."[64] Eric Guerin rolled to safety while Your Host struggled to rise, his right leg shattered at the shoulder in four places.[65] Exercise rider Tuffy Morlan raced to him: "There he stood, broken and in horrible pain, but his funny cockeyed head was up and he whinnied at me, a faint desperate sound. It was the first time he had ever asked me for help. I knew he needed me then and I could do nothing but take him by the head and weep. I don't think I ever felt so empty and lost as at that moment."[66]

For Your Host, one miraculous journey had ended and another begun. Lloyds of London paid his enormous insurance, assumed ownership, and embarked on desperate measures to save the colt's life. With his leg set and stall packed in sand, the proud colt hung on as the months ticked by, and slowly he began to mend. When the cast was removed, his right leg was twisted and shortened, requiring "an elaborate brace . . . to hobble about,"[67] but three legs were sound and the young colt could cover mares. After standing a year in California, Your Host was sold to a New Jersey syndicate, and Mrs. Richard C. duPont purchased shares.

On April 4, 1957, Maid of Flight lay down in a Kentucky stall and gave birth to a near black son of Your Host, with no distinguishing features save white anklets on his dark hind legs. Free of the anomalies that plagued his sire, the new colt was nonetheless unpromising—unusually small, painfully thin, and outwardly fragile. Reportedly, Claiborne Farm's general manager Bull Hancock was concerned. "Nothing wrong with this foal, is there?" he called to the foreman. "No sir," came the reply, "the vet says he's just fine."[68]

Days passed slowly at Claiborne Farm, while mares and foals lazed in spring pasture—the mares grazing on calcium-rich bluegrass, the foals stretching their legs to romp not far from their mothers' side. From his office window, Bull Hancock watched, noticing the hard clean limbs and high spirits of Maid of Flight's undersized colt—goading older companions into games of tag, and persisting long after they had stopped.[69]

Weeks later, mother and son returned to Mrs. duPont's Maryland farm. Known as Woodstock, the tranquil farm would become the colt's home for twenty-six years, and Mrs. duPont, his lifelong friend. She was there from the start, appearing daily with dogs in tow, bearing sugar and carrots for her equine companions. In time, the brown colt knew her voice, nickering on sight, and poking her pockets for the sweets he always favored. "The horse that love built," one journalist wrote.[70] Come summer, he was registered and given his name. Unknowingly, the small foal now carried the name of one of his great ancestor's proudest achievements, the 1877 Kelso Gold Cup.

Kelso winning the 1963 Gulfstream Handicap by three and a half lengths.

Chapter Two

The Mark of a Champion

THE POST WAR YEARS of the 1950s marked a national decade of prosperity and promise for American citizens. The nation brimmed with confidence and rapid economic expansion. Rising wages fueled consumption, swelling the middle class and the reach of television to the majority of American homes. Through the grainy images of a black- and-white screen, I witnessed the drama of human history and the storied exploits of Kelso's career. Kelso was six months old the day the Space Age began with the Soviet launch of Sputnik I, the first satellite to orbit the earth. That fall, he was weaned from his mother. On January 1, 1958, the official birthday of all thoroughbreds, the nine-month old colt became a yearling.

While Woodstock Farm developed to meet the needs of a thoroughbred operation, Kelso and the Bohemia string were stabled in Middletown, Delaware, under the charge of part-time trainer, Dr. John Lee. Come summer, the yearling's education began. Accustomed to handling, grooming, and leading since birth, "breaking" was a natural progression. The young colt learned to "longe," circling his handler at the end of a long line, responding to voice, pole taps, and the line itself, gradually moving through gaits on command. He was tacked and led, then mounted and led again, balancing anew under the weight of a rider. Eventually, the youth could move through his paces, steered by a mounted rider. But patient as the process was, Kelso proved intractable, kicking, biting, and tossing his riders, asserting his will at every turn. With little to lose, the scrawny, obstreperous colt was gelded.[1]

Assigned a mature lead pony named Spray, Kelso began training on the track of Bayard Sharp's adjoining farm, walking, trotting, and galloping beside his companion. Eventually, he ran alone; stretching his legs while his rider urged him forward. Morning workouts became routine, sometimes jogging, sometimes running, building strength at increasing distance and speed. But the young gelding remained a handful. On New Year's Day 1959, Kelso turned two.

Delayed by an injured stifle,[2] eight months passed before Kelso appeared for his two-year-old debut on September 4, 1959. Sent to the post for a six-furlong Maiden Special at Atlantic City, the green colt broke late and last, "nearly stumbling to his knees"[3] as he bolted forward. Seventh at the quarter, sixth at the half, and still five lengths behind in fourth place with a furlong remaining, he flew down the track to collar the leaders and win going away by a length and a quarter. He had broken his maiden first out, and done so with class and courage.

Two subsequent races followed that month—both allowance purses at Atlantic City. Kelso rallied from fourth to finish second in the first, then lost a seven-furlong duel with Windy Sands to place second by three-quarters of a length in his last start of the season, despite striking an ankle. The small colt had performed surprisingly well, but Lee feared he would "bow" a tendon, a tearing of fibers that could end his career.[4] Kelso was returned to the farm to mature and grow, and Mrs. duPont advised to find a buyer.

By February 1960, Bohemia had expanded to nine horses. Dr. Lee recommended a full-time trainer, and resigned to expand his veterinary practice. When experienced horseman Carl Hanford applied for the position, Mrs. duPont recognized her complement—a modest, soft-spoken, conservative trainer, committed to patient development, and attentive to the psyche of the equine mind.

That month, while Kentucky Derby hopefuls emerged, Hanford took charge of Bohemia's string. Years later, many would question why the future champion never appeared in the Triple Crown classics. Carl Hanford explains:

> Nobody knew Kelso was a Derby caliber horse. He wintered on the farm in Maryland—he probably galloped there some—but he didn't begin training until Delaware [on Sharpe's farm] just before I got there. Kelso wasn't ready. He was too undeveloped-too light in weight- and it would have been rushing him too much to run a mile and a quarter the first Saturday in May.[5]

In truth, the new trainer knew little about Kelso when he arrived, and given the youth's ill manners, had no way to judge his merits. "No one wanted to ride him,"[6] Hanford recalls, and by default, the newest, lightest rider on the farm had been given the task. Invariably, as each workout ended, Kelso wheeled in the opposite direction, swinging both reins to one side of his neck, and rendering his rider helpless. "Most horses wheel on their way to the track," Hanford explains. "Kelso was just feeling good. He wanted more work."[7] Hanford obliged, employing Lionel LeFavre for two weeks to tame the gelding's unruly behavior.[8]

A running martingale (strap forked at the chest and attached to each rein by a sliding ring) was introduced to foil Kelso's rein pitching, LeFavre stayed on his back, and the new rider worked him harder, "going out with him for half-hour at a clip each day."[9] Within two weeks, he was easier—though never easy—to manage.

"He was a tough horse to gallop—very tough," Hanford recalls. "He was so strong, he'd run off with an inexperienced rider." Come spring, when the stable moved to Delaware Park, Bohemia's Dick Jenkins, a former bronc rider and Quarter Horse jockey,[10] became Kelso's regular exercise rider for the duration of the gelding's career. The headstrong horse proved a challenge, but under Jenkin's skill and Hanford's patient care, his assertive conduct became an asset to tap. Above all else, the new trainer observed: Kelso wanted to run.

Nine months had elapsed since his last race when Kelso appeared for his three-year-old debut on June 22, 1960. The Triple Crown races had been run and won; the names of Venetian Way, Bally Ache, and Celtic Ash etched in permanent record. By that date in his own three-year-old season, Man o' War was a living legend, only four months removed from his last glorious triumph over Triple Crown winner Sir Barton in the Kenilworth Gold Cup. For Kelso, it was only the beginning.

Prior to the race, Hanford received a call from Mrs. duPont. "I have good news," she said. "Someone wants to buy Kelso." "I wouldn't do that if I were you," Hanford replied. "If this horse runs the way he's been working, he'll win."[11]

Hopes that Kelso would fill out and grow hadn't materialized. Still small and ungainly, the three-year-old stood just a shade over 15 hands, a thin neck protruding from a bony frame. What height he had was concentrated in long lean legs, suggesting a petite, deerlike appearance. On that Wednesday in June, the United States launched two satellites from one rocket to orbit in space. On the same day, virtually unnoticed in the fifth race at Monmouth Park, an unpretentious brown gelding launched a career that would rocket him to stardom.

None could have dreamed that the small gelding whose "only attraction. . . . was the piteous appeal of an emaciated Oliver Twist"[12] would one day emerge a national hero. Kelso broke fast, rushed to the front, and never looked back, winning by ten widening lengths, tripping the timer in 1:10 for the six furlongs, and besting a mediocre field to bring home the $4,500 purse. Public attention was focused on two-year-olds, with the long shot Chinchilla taking the five-and-a-half-furlong Tyro Stakes. In third place was a little-known colt named Carry Back, destined to be one of the toughest rivals Kelso would face in his eight-year career.

Carl Hanford was confident Bohemia had a racehorse, and three weeks later on July 16, Kelso appeared for a one-mile contest on the Aqueduct oval. On that Saturday, an Irish horse, Tharp, scored headlines when he captured the featured Sheepshead Bay Handicap on the turf. Earlier that day, unnoticed by the public, another horse caught press attention. The last paragraph in the *Times* account of Tharp's triumph records the following:

> KELSO RUNS 1:34 1/5 MILE
> The Bohemia Stable's Kelso ran the fastest mile on record for a 3-year old in New York in taking the first division of a $4,500 allowance event. This was the fifth race on the program. The gelding, who won the last time out by 10 lengths in a six-furlong race, was the favorite this time.[13]

The little-known gelding had run the fastest mile ever recorded by a three-year-old in 295 years of New York racing; the fastest since thoroughbreds first competed in 1665 on the Salisbury Plain of Long Island.[14] The young horse had gone to the front and stayed there, burning fractions of 0:23 for the first quarter mile, 0:45 1/5 for the half, 1:09 for six furlongs and 1:34 1/5 for the mile. And, as the racing chart noted, he had "won easily" by twelve expanding lengths.

With new confidence in Kelso's prowess, the stable plunged forward, putting up the late fee to start him a week later in Chicago's $100,000 Arlington Classic, a one-mile test against the best three-year-olds in America. It was a big leap for the inexperienced colt, and he finished eighth in the twelve-horse field. The talented T.V. Lark emerged victorious, defeating John William and Venetian Way, the Kentucky Derby champion. Kelso was off poorly and "buffeted badly,"[15] hopelessly blocked from start to finish. To all but connections, the decision to run the gelding seemed premature. Jockey Steve Brooks told Carl Hanford: "I don't know what kind of horse you've got. I never had a chance to let him run."[16] He needn't have said a word. Hanford had seen it all through binoculars. Kelso returned to the barn as fresh and eager to run as when he started.

Belief in his horse unshaken, Hanford sent Kelso out eleven days later to contest the mile-and-a-sixteenth Choice Stakes at Monmouth Park, his first effort beyond a mile. This time, Kelso didn't disappoint, romping to his first stakes victory by seven lengths "with speed to spare." In front all the way, he breezed by three-quarters in 1:09 3/5, and crossed the finish line one-fifth of a second off the track record. As recorded by the *New York Times*: "After one grin over his right shoulder an eighth of a mile out, Hartack eased his mount inside the sixteenth pole. Had he not, Kelso easily could have set a track record." The experienced Bill Hartack himself was impressed. The story continued: "This was the first time I had ridden this horse in a stakes. . . . He's a young horse, but he seems very willing. In my estimation, that makes him a pretty good one."[17]

Still unnoticed by all but the press and race fans devoted enough to follow a midweek schedule, Kelso had launched an eleven-race winning streak as sensational as any in the long history of the sport.

A month passed before Kelso appeared again, this time in the ninety-first running of the one-mile Jerome Handicap, the second oldest race in America. Unable to reach Bill Hartack,

Hanford contacted Bones LaBoyne, agent for George Edward (Eddie) Arcaro. "Sure," Bones replied, "We'll ride that bale of wire."[18] Years later, Joe Hirsch would record: "It was a partnership that was to flourish to such an extent, that before he retired in the early Spring of 1962, Arcaro, who had known unparalleled moments of glory aboard Citation, Bold Ruler, Nashua and so many other cracks, was to refer to Kelso as the best horse he had ever ridden."[19]

The Jerome itself was a corker. Coming from ninth place in a thirteen-horse field, Kelso closed swiftly in the last eighth to nip Careless John by a head at the wire. His time of 1:34 4/5 was the fastest Jerome in the history of the race. In winning the historic event, Kelso had run himself into good company. He had joined Aristides, first winner of the Kentucky Derby, and Fair Play, father of Man o' War. He had broken Bold Ruler's record, and bettered the times of Coaltown, Tom Fool, and Intentionally, world-record holder for the distance. Though it failed to make headlines, for the first time, Kelso was featured on the front page of the Sunday *New York Times* sports section.

Eleven days later on September 13, Kelso was back, this time for the mile-and-an-eighth Discovery Handicap at Aqueduct. "Left at the post by a good two lengths,"[20] Kelso swerved at the break and was last among eight horses entering the clubhouse turn. Advancing to fifth on the backstretch and fourth on the far turn, he shot into the lead with a quarter mile to go, drawing away from Careless John to win by a length and a quarter at the wire.

It was Wednesday, and racing was restricted to the fourth page of the sports section, but this time the gelding drew headlines:

KELSO'S RECORD CLOCKING CAPTURES DISCOVERY HANDICAP AT AQUEDUCT

COLT CLOSES FAST FROM LAST PLACE

KELSO SETS A TRACK RECORD OF 1:48 2/5 IN 1 1/8-
MILE RACE[21]

As confirmed by the chart, "Start good for all but Kelso," the
gelding had been left at the break but catapulted, undaunted, to a
record-breaking finish. In the winner's circle, Arcaro leapt from his
mount and confronted Hanford: "What the hell kind of horse is
this? I had him beat three times, and he still won the race."[22] To
reporters, he said: "If he didn't have the speed to get through every
time I asked him, we would have been last."[23]

After two trips on the gelding, Arcaro was convinced he could
tackle the nation's best horses in the upcoming Woodward
Stakes—high praise considering he had the mount on Sword
Dancer, reigning Woodward champion and Horse of the Year.
"He's good enough to rate a chance at them now," Arcaro said, "and
if it can't be the Woodward, it'll come later in the year."[24] Kelso
wasn't entered in the Woodward, but as predicted, his chance
would come.

There is an adage among old horsemen: "The most publicized
races are run in the spring, the truly great races in the fall."[25] On
September 23 with Arcaro aboard, Sword Dancer stormed to his
second Woodward triumph, leaving Horse of the Year contenders
Dotted Swiss, Bald Eagle, and T.V. Lark in his wake.

On Wednesday, September 28, Kelso reappeared. And this
time, Bohemia upped the ante. The race was the Lawrence
Realization, the mile-and-five-furlong, three-year-old "test of
heart." First won by mighty Salvator in 1889, the list of winners
reads like a parade of champions from the first half of the twentieth century: Sysonby, Man o' War, Gallant Fox, Twenty Grand,
Whirlaway, and Alsab. It includes Count Fleet's father, Reigh
Count, and his son Counterpoint. On this day, the name of his
grandson would be added to the roster as well.

It was a bold move, asking the son of Your Host to run a half-mile further than he had ever raced before. And, proving they knew their horse, it was a move that would propel the gelding into history. As recorded by the *Times*:

> Kelso Equals 40-Year-Old Track Mark at Belmont Park
>
> Tompion is Next in $56,000 Race
>
> Kelso, 1-2, Takes Lawrence Realization in 2:40 4/5, Winning by 4 1/2 Lengths
>
> Kelso moved into the top rank of stake-winners at Belmont Park yesterday when he equaled Man o' War's 40 year-old track record in winning the Lawrence Realization by four and one-half lengths. Eddie Arcaro. . . . took a firm hold of Kelso with a sixteenth of a mile to go. Had he gone to a drive, the son of Your Host and Maid of Flight might easily have set a track mark.
>
> Turning into the stretch, Kelso moved to an easy four-length lead on the rail. Down to the wire he never was threatened. At the finish, he seemed to be running well inside himself.[26]

So well inside himself, the track photo revealed his ears pricked, reveling in the sights and sounds of the revered old track as he gamboled under the wire. In his first outing beyond a mile and an eighth, Kelso had run a mile and a half faster than all but one rendition of the Belmont Stakes.[27] He had left Tompion, winner of the historic Travers, in his wake.

The Blood-Horse minced no praise:

> The Realization erased what little doubt remained about Kelso's quality. The gelded son of Your Host had done almost everything asked of him up to the

Realization, but the question of distance remained. After a mile and 5 furlongs in 2:40 4/5, which equaled Man o' War's 40-year-old track record, the final doubt was removed and a real runner stood out in clear focus for all to see.

Kelso stayed off the pace and simply cantered around his field when ready to score. His mile-and-a-quarter time was 2:02 1/5, his mile-and-a-half time 2:27 3/5, and his final time, eased up to a jog, equaled Man o' War's mark.[28]

The Thoroughbred Record was equally generous: "By the grace of Arcaro's decision to ease up Kelso in the final 30 yards or so. . . . Man o' War's longstanding record at Belmont of 2:40 4/5 for a mile and five furlongs still stands today. . . . Kelso unquestionably would have smashed the record had Arcaro ridden him out, or even hustled him a bit in the closing phases of the one-sided event."[29]

With this stunning performance the young gelding had run himself into the balloting for three-year-old honors. Again, the experts had taken notice, and again, most of the public missed it.

It was time to test Arcaro's opinion. Bohemia submitted a late fee to confront On-and-On, Dotted Swiss, and three-year-old T.V. Lark in Chicago's fall feature, the mile-and-a-quarter Hawthorne Gold Cup. It would be the first time Kelso faced older horses, and his first voyage on an "off" track. "Squeezed back"[30] on the rail, and assailed by mud from every angle, Kelso never flinched. On the far turn, he swept to the leaders, and with three-eighths remaining, drew even. From there it was a romp to the wire, as Kelso sailed home six lengths on top "with speed to spare," clocking an "excellent"[31] 2:02 on the deep and slippery surface. T.V. Lark was eighth, unable to handle the going, but the two were destined to meet again. The mud-spattered dark bay was draped in roses, and for the first time, claimed front-page headlines in the sports section of the Sunday *Times*: KELSO SCORES. The public may have been asking "Kelso who?" but the press had clearly caught on. In a feature article, the *Times* quoted Arcaro: "[Kelso] ran like the great horse we think he is and this proves it."[32] Bill Surface of the *The Thoroughbred Record* touched on the same theme: "Winning seven of eight races as a three-year-old does not qualify Kelso as a great horse. It may not even earn him the year-end championship in his division. But it has the curious wondering out loud if the gelded son of Your Host-Maid of Flight, by Count Fleet, could have been a 'great one' by now had he been campaigned more heavily as a two-year-old in 1959 and also earlier this season."[33]

With little left to prove, Kelso's defining performance that year was yet to come. Horses of past centuries had raced in four-mile heats with scarcely thirty minutes between. To many, this was the "heroic age"[34] of American racing, and it lasted until the Civil War. By 1860, "the American ideal of running mature horses over an appreciable distance had begun to slip."[35] English "dashes" took root, particularly in the industrialized north, as did the racing of two- and three-year-old horses.[36] Southern racing remained the last stronghold of America's endurance tradition, but that, too, would perish with the collapse of Charleston and fall of the South.[37] A century later, four-mile races were a thing of the past, and only a handful of two-mile events remained—the last vestiges of a bygone era.

The Jockey Club Gold Cup was the crown jewel—the ultimate test in American racing—the mark, and often the making, of a champion. In his classic work, *The History of Thoroughbred Racing in America*, William H. P. Robertson writes: "The Jockey Club Gold Cup . . . at 2 miles under weight for age conditions, is as definitive a test of intrinsic class as there is in the United States."[38]

First run in 1919 at a mile-and-a-half, the race was a walkover, with Purchase having only to jog around the track to claim victory. The second running saw Man o' War beat Damask by fifteen lengths, setting a new American record for the mile and a half. In 1921, the race was extended to two miles, and remained at that distance for fifty-four years, until reduced to its original length ten years after Kelso's retirement.[39] During that time it served as center stage for some of the best horses and best races ever witnessed in North America. Triple Crown winners Gallant Fox, War Admiral, Whirlaway, and Citation included the race in their conquests. Reigh Count, and grandsons One Count and Counterpoint, were victorious, as were Belmont winners Nashua, Gallant Man, and Sword Dancer. In later years, Buckpasser, Damascus, and Forego would triumph. In sum, no less than seventeen Horse of the Year champions claimed the two-mile prize since balloting began in 1936. The Jockey Club Gold Cup was no race for pretenders.

On October 29, 1960, the stage was set for the most decisive race of the year. The track was "sloppy" as eight contenders waded to the post. Among them were the finest distance runners in the nation. Bald Eagle, leading contender for Horse of the Year honors, had the added advantage of a running mate, Tooth and Nail. Don Poggio, an Argentine import, excelled at long routes, having won three New York classics at a mile and a half or more. Dotted Swiss owned the distance prizes of California, while Harmonizing had decisively bested both Bald Eagle and Sword Dancer in the mile-and-a-half Man o' War Stakes. For all that distance talent, it promised to be a horse race.

Tooth and Nail performed his job well, soaring to a fifteen-length lead in the first three-quarters. Behind him, no one was fooled. When the pacesetter faltered, Don Poggio seized command. Kelso went with him, lapped on his shoulder, while Dotted Swiss stalked a length behind. For a half-mile they ran as a pack—Don Poggio and Kelso heads apart on the lead. On the far turn, Bald Eagle menaced briefly on the rail. Don Poggio let out a notch; Kelso went with him. By the quarter pole, they'd opened seven lengths on the field. Together, they churned into the stretch—Don Poggio straining mightily to shake his rival, Kelso glued to his side. With 300 yards remaining, Arcaro raised his whip and let it fall—twice. Under a furious drive, Don Poggio staved off the onslaught, but in the end was no match for the stouthearted gelding. With 200 yards remaining, Kelso bounded away, opening daylight "without need of urging," splashing under the wire three and a half lengths ahead of his foe. It was another ten lengths back to Bald Eagle, and an additional fifteen lengths to Dotted Swiss.

Kelso's victory was decisive, his time, unbelievable. On a track deep in standing water, Kelso had unleashed the fastest two miles in North American history, easily shattering Nashua's mark by a full second. Charles Hatton recorded: "Kelso returned to scale looking perfectly capable of duplicating his splendid performance that very afternoon if necessary. The day was rather chill, and steam was rising from horses chests and loins . . . but Kelso would scarcely have blown out a match."[40]

Eddie Arcaro agreed: "At the end I was breathing harder than he was."[41] For the second time that month, Kelso captured Sunday headlines, and this time even his appearance drew respect:

KELSO WINS

Favorite Sets U. S. Record for Two Miles in Gold Cup

Mrs. Richard C. duPont's lean, hard-muscled, 3-year old gelding Kelso set an American track record of 3:19 2/5 yesterday when he won the two-mile Jockey Club Gold Cup by three and one-half lengths in the slop at

Aqueduct. The dark brown, almost black, son of Your Host and the Count Fleet mare, Maid of Flight, also entered a strong set of credentials for horse-of-the-year honors.[42]

Mike Casale of the *Thoroughbred Record* agreed:

> Hail 1960's Horse of the Year—Kelso, who in my opinion, gloriously earned the exalted honor. . . on October 29th when the brilliant three-year-old. . . splashed to a resoundingly popular triumph in the 42nd edition of the two-mile, weight-for-age Jockey Club Gold Cup. By way of further demonstrating his enormous class, Mrs. Richard C. duPont's home-bred covered the long journey in slop in 3:19 2/5, setting a new track and American record for the distance.[43]

Three days later, a glamorous young war hero was elected President. At month's end, Kelso was voted 1960 Horse of the Year and Three Year Old Champion, the first three-year-old in history to achieve that honor without a Triple Crown race to his credit. He had streaked from nowhere to stardom in four short months—winning eight of nine starts—equaling or breaking four records—at distances ranging from one mile to two. In his annual profile of the year's top horses, Charles Hatton wrote: "He scattered his presumptuous rivals like a fox scattering a barnyard of chickens and broke or equaled time marks with unpremeditated abandon."[43]

Kelso returned to Woodstock Farm to rest and prepare for his four-year-old campaign. The small son of Maid of Flight and the California Comet had magically sprouted wings.

Kelso winning the Suburban Handicap carrying 133 pounds. Only the second horse to win the ancient handicap twice, he was the first to do so under such heavy weights. (Bob Coglianese)

The Weight of History

G reat is a word used cautiously in racing, with respect for tradition, and deference to measures passed down through centuries of competition. To an impressionable child rooted in history, "great" was a magical word, evoking images of mythic figures that I had been born too late to witness. In 1960, there was no Marlboro Cup or VISA Triple Crown, no corporate sponsorship or media hype to whet the appetite of a willing audience. Old-timers spoke of greatness in hushed tones, and disciples of the sport reserved judgment until the body of proof was in.

In 1978, when trainer Bud Delp declared Spectacular Bid "the greatest horse ever to look through a bridle," his premature boast was akin to heresy.[1] That same year, minutes after Affirmed captured the Triple Crown, owner Louis Wolfson embraced the historic precedent: "Yes, [Affirmed is] a great three-year old. But I want to see him run at four before I call him great overall."[2]

At three, Kelso was spectacular. He won at one mile, and he won at two. He triumphed on fast tracks, and prevailed in the mud. He won as fortune demanded—on the lead, from the middle, or flying from behind. He encountered good luck, bad luck, and once, no luck at all. But when it mattered at the wire, it was his head in front. He defeated his own generation, and moved up to crush the best of the next, twice. As Charles Hatton would write the following year, "A great racehorse never has an excuse."[3] He was referring to Kelso.

By 1961, only two measures of a great horse remained—to win under imposed handicaps, and to prevail when pushed to the last ounce of strength. To appreciate Kelso's achievements that year, it is necessary to understand the history of "handicap" racing, beginning where it started at the close of the Civil War.

With the fall of the South came the decline of Southern racing; the destruction of farms, crops, tracks and breeding centers. With all resources exhausted, many a fleet thoroughbred died on the battlefield. The industrialized North emerged as the sport's epicenter, and the public assumed "the dominant role"[4] in shaping the Sport of Kings. In an urban culture, racing emerged as a spectator sport, a source of entertainment for the new working class. "Stepped-up programs"[5] of more races at shorter distances required additional prize money, and more money, greater attendance. In 1877, the American Jockey Club was forced to accept that "the pure concept of sport for sport's sake had to be tempered with the realities of economic necessity." Soon after, gambling "exchanged its stool in the corner for a seat at the main table."[6]

With wagering came new rules of engagement. "While spectators might admire a runner that was obviously superior to his opposition, such a stalwart was a poor business proposition—the odds were too short to bet on him, and it was foolhardy to bet against him. Moreover, other owners tended to avoid crack rivals, reducing the size of the field. To counteract this aspect, various artificial devices were introduced to manipulate a horse's natural form."[7] Thus emerged "handicapping"—an intentional effort to slow the best horse, and provide each contestant a sporting chance of victory.

From the time a horse turns four, until the end of his career, most races, with the exception of fall classics, are run under "handicap" conditions. Unlike the three-year-old Triple Crown, in which all horses carry the same weight, handicap races require horses to carry different amounts of weight to compensate for differences in natural ability. Weight is assigned by the Racing Secretary, and added to the jockey's weight in the form of lead slabs carried in cloth pads under the saddle. If a horse is assigned 130 pounds, and his rider and equipment weigh 110, twenty pounds of lead must be packed on the spine to make up the difference.

To the average observer, a few extra pounds may seem insignificant on a large animal. To the knowledgeable, however, those few pounds exact a heavy toll. Eddie Arcaro, the "Master" himself, called 130 pounds the "breaking point," and he would know. In 1950, he tried three times to bring the mighty Citation home in front under 130 pounds, and three times he failed.[8] A time-tested formula reveals the relationship between weight and distance:[9]

> At 1 mile: 2 pounds = 1 length
> At 1 1/4 miles: 2 pounds = 1 1/2 lengths

In short, a little extra weight goes a long way toward effecting outcome. The reason is found in anatomy. The spine of the horse works in unison with abdominal muscles, which in turn affect stride. The greater the weight on the spine, the greater the strain on the abdomen and effort required to stride freely.[10] As weight increases, bone, muscle, heart, and lungs are taxed prematurely, oxygen debt takes an earlier toll, and tiring results more quickly. The longer the race, or faster the pace, the greater the effect of weight on outcome.[11]

The amount or proportion of lead is itself a factor. "Lead weight is dead weight," referring to its motionless position on the horse's spine. Rider weight is "live weight," raised off the runner's back and positioned low over the neck and shoulder where it is more easily carried: urging, pumping, propelling the horse forward.

Last but not least is an often overlooked factor: the size of the horse itself. The three-year old Secretariat stood 17 hands at the shoulder, and weighed 1,250 pounds. Forego, the last of the great weight bearers, was so oversized he barely fit in a starting gate. At three, Kelso stood 15 hands, 3 1/2 inches, and weighed 870 pounds.[12] By four, he had gained half an inch and 100 pounds. There he stayed, never exceeding 970 pounds in racing condition.[13] Applying load-to-weight ratios, we can infer the following: 130 pounds on Kelso was equal to 147 pounds on the average 1,100-pound horse, 168 on a horse the size of Secretariat or Forego.[14] Using height as the index instead: 130 pounds on Kelso compared to 138 on a horse four inches taller.[15] Logic alone dictates the following: it is harder for a small horse to carry 130 pounds than it is for a large one.

By 1960, the ability to prevail under imposed loads had become a requisite measure of greatness—a bridge to the past that would define Kelso for the remainder of his career. In *The History of Thoroughbred Racing in America*, William H. P. Robertson writes:

> There are so many factors that can affect the performance of a racehorse . . . that to evaluate a thoroughbred according to any single criterion is ridiculous. Time, the most popular basis, is a fickle jade who blows hot and cold at track to track from day to day. The significance of money won is subject to an even wider variety of interpretation. If one particular standard must be used, the preference of the author is for weight: 132 pounds is 132 pounds, at Santa Anita or Saratoga, Woodbine or the Fair Grounds, and it was the same burden in 1910 that it will be in 1980.[16]

Historian Charles Hatton echoed the sentiment: "Weight brings them all together. . . for a pound remains a pound from year to year and century to century."[17]

R omantic notions endured as well. History suggested that no horse, no matter how swift or strong, could wear the mantle of greatness, until pushed, at least once, to the edge of endurance and beyond—and not found wanting for courage. Such had been the defining moment for Man o' War—not his hundred-length triumph over Hoodwink, nor his effortless seven-length conquest of Triple Crown winner Sir Barton—but his length-and-a-half victory over John P. Grier, the little colt who dueled him every step of the way in record-breaking fractions, and with 200 yards remaining, pushed his head in front. Never before had Man o' War been headed, and the crowd sensed he was beaten. But Big Red didn't flinch. With one terrible surge, the spent, foam-flecked champion overtook the gallant Grier, and the last remaining question was answered—Man o' War was not without courage.[18] The bar had been set for those who followed.

K elso was in California as 1960 drew to a close, preparing for the prestigious Santa Anita Maturity. Only three days shy of the New Year and his official fourth birthday, he reinjured his right stifle in a morning drill, forcing a return to Woodstock Farm, and cancellation of his winter campaign. By February, he was pronounced fit, and sent to the Aiken Training Center in South Carolina to ready for a spring debut. By March, he had created a stir:

> Aiken, S.C. "I think Kelso is the best horse I have ever seen since Man o' War." The speaker was Howard Hoffman, the affable sixty-one-year-old veteran who

trains for L. L. Haggin II, President of Keeneland race course. Hoffman has been around the race tracks since 1913, and he has seen the best ones of his time. . . "It just proves you can't judge a book by its cover. He'll go from a mile to 2 miles. He's done it. And I once saw him breeze a Belmont workout in 1:10. . . I haven't seen the equal of him since Man o' War."[19]

Two months passed before Kelso returned to competition, and during that time, the world balanced on a tenuous thread— between hope one minute, holocaust the next; between the best and basest of the human spirit. On April 12, a smiling Russian cosmonaut hurtled through space in orbital flight, breaking forever our bondage to earth. Five days later, 1,300 Cuban exiles launched an ill-fated invasion of Cuba at the Bay of Pigs. The Cold War plunged to a frigid low. On that same day, Kelso's sire, Your Host, was destroyed, following a debilitating injury to his right stifle. Fittingly, the courageous stallion was buried alongside valiant John P. Grier.[20]

On May 4, thirteen Freedom Riders boarded two buses in Washington, D.C., to challenge southern segregation of interstate buses and terminals. The following day, Alan Shepard shot above the atmosphere to become the first American in space. A new race gripped the nation. Just one day later, on May 6, a "Cinderella horse" obtained in lieu of a $300 debt, launched a flight of his own, winning the Kentucky Derby with a heart-stopping rush from behind. His name was Carry Back, and through the sweeping reach of national networks, he emerged as America's new equine idol. The public loved the gritty colt, and I, too, fell under the spell of his celebrated quest for the Triple Crown.

On May 19, 1961, the eve of the Preakness Stakes, the eyes of the media focused on Maryland. That same day, Kelso emerged in New York for his four-year-old debut.

At the age of four, Kelso cruises to his tenth straight victory in the 1961 Suburban Handicap, an event inaugurated at Sheepshead Bay in 1884. (Bert & Richard Morgan)

Chapter Four

The Burden of Proof

K ELSO'S AUSPICIOUS RETURN WAS buried in a New York byline. The event was a seven-furlong dash, a "tightener" for a horse that had been away from the races too long. Kelso broke fifth in the field of seven, stalked the front runners, and "moved on the outside with such power that his victory was predictable an eighth of a mile from home." It was his seventh straight victory, and the gelding "took up just where he left off last year."[1]

The following day, Carry Back captured the Preakness Stakes with another signature sprint from behind. In New York, the public was seized by Belmont fever, and Carry Back's date with Triple Crown destiny. Kelso, too, was stabled at Belmont Park, but in the celebrity's shadow few seemed to notice. Few, that is, except newly appointed Racing Secretary, Tommy Trotter. When weights were announced for the gelding's next start, the May 30 Metropolitan Handicap, Kelso was assigned 130 pounds—130 pounds following a seven-month layoff and one minor victory. Again, I was reminded of the Gold Cup hero, and again I was drawn to the historic dimension of his journey. Few horses in modern history have been asked to shoulder so heavy a burden, fewer still as the baseline for their handicap career. Tommy Trotter had set an awfully high bar for an awfully spare horse—in a mighty important race.

The Metropolitan Handicap is the first jewel in the Handicap Triple Crown, a grouping of three historic events, the Metropolitan, Suburban, and Brooklyn Handicaps, which predate the twentieth century. Widely considered the most difficult achievement in American racing, a high price is exacted for consecutive scores. As victories mount, so does weight, until the odds of winning diminish. Between 1891 and 1961, eight horses had triumphed in the nation's oldest Triple Crown—the Kentucky Derby, Preakness, and Belmont Stakes—exclusive to three-year-olds carrying equal weight. But since 1891, only two, Whisk Broom II and Tom Fool, had captured the more elusive prize, the demanding Handicap Crown.

Other horses had triumphed in two jewels, but failed, or failed to attempt, the third. One of the best was Equipoise, two-time winner of the Metropolitan. By two, the "Chocolate Soldier" was legend, hurtling out of two shoes in a sea of mud to nip Twenty Grand at the wire. Following injuries at three, Equipoise stormed back at four, seizing his first seven starts, including the Metropolitan Mile. By year's end, he had won ten of fourteen races, and was voted 1932 Handicap Champion and Horse of the Year. At five, he repeated the feat, reeling off seven straight victories in nine starts, including a second Metropolitan, and the Suburban Handicap carrying 132 pounds. Once again, the "Chocolate Soldier" was named Handicap Champion and Horse of the Year. At six, he carried 130 pounds five times in six starts, winning three, and placing in his third Metropolitan, disqualified from victory for bumping in the stretch. For the third straight season, Equipoise was elected Champion Handicap Horse. Numerous winners had come and gone in the interim, including Tom Fool, Native Dancer, Nashua, Swaps, and six three-year-old Triple Crown champions, but Carl Hanford remained convinced: Equipoise was the greatest racehorse he'd ever seen.

Twenty-seven years later, another Metropolitan loomed, and another brown soldier prepared to face the greatest challenge of his career. With one race under his belt and 130 pounds on his back, few were scared off by 1960's Horse of the Year. Ten horses paraded to the post for the one-mile contest, toting burdens of 108 pounds to Kelso's 130. In effect, Kelso was conceding two to eleven lengths to his rivals. To this day, I remember the account.

All Hands, under 117 pounds, broke alertly, followed by Mail Order and Conestoga. When Conestoga faded, the lightly weighted Sweet William moved up to challenge, as All Hands continued powerfully on the lead. Kelso was eighth, hopelessly blocked from the start through the backstretch, and still seventh with only a quarter mile remaining. When the field turned for home, it was All Hands by three and flying. Kelso, bottled in seventh, appeared beaten. Desperate for running room, Arcaro changed course in the stretch and cut inside. The hole closed. With 220 yards to go, three horses blocking him, and All Hands winging three lengths in front, Arcaro did the unthinkable—he checked his mount and pulled him from the inside of the track to the out, circling Mail Order, Sweet William, and Careless John in one sweep. Finally, he was clear.

With 100 yards and thirteen strides remaining, All Hands sailed three lengths in front, out of range for all but a speeding bullet. Arcaro took aim. Kelso exploded . . . With two jumps left, he caught the frontrunner. In the final jump he passed him, flashing under the wire a neck in front. His time for the last quarter was blistering—23 4/5 seconds—though that fraction hardly conveyed his final speed. The truth is, we'll never know how fast Kelso ran that last 100 yards, as races simply weren't timed that way. Eddie Arcaro estimated eleven seconds flat for the final furlong.[2] Carl Hanford says: "He probably did." All we know for certain is this: In that final sixteenth of a mile, Kelso ran a hole in the wind.

Reporters called it "miraculous,"[3] "spectacular,"[4] "never-to-be-for-gotten."[5] Bob Horwood of the *Morning Telegraph* reviewed the film more than twenty times, concluding: "Had Kelso been anything less than a great horse, it is virtually certain that he would not have finished closer than fourth."[6]

> As he straightened away, Kelso seemed, to the naked eye and in the films, to gather himself like a cat, then spring. He continued his drive with relentless fury, his stride so long that his belly seemed to almost touch the ground. There are points when the stopped film shows that Kelso had both his forelegs and his hind legs fully extended in the style seen in the old-time sporting prints.[7]

Carl Hanford, himself, couldn't believe what he had witnessed, but under the watchful eye of Tommy Trotter, he was cautious: "I guess his next race will be the Whitney. I don't want him breaking down with weight, so I'm not planning on handicaps."[8] Years later, Hanford would recall that race as a turning point—the moment he realized that Kelso, not Equipoise, was the greatest horse he'd ever seen.[9]

A week later, Carry Back sustained a minor injury, and failed in his attempt to capture the Triple Crown. True to his word, Hanford sent Kelso back for the thirty-third running of the mile-and-an-eighth Whitney Stakes. Despite what he'd told reporters, the Bohemia team shared a secret: Kelso had been pointed toward one goal since February—a Triple Crown victory he'd been denied at three.

With weights for the second jewel of the crown unannounced, Hanford's instructions barely needed stating—"win by the small-est margin possible." Seven horses paraded to the post, with Kelso again shouldering 130 pounds. But this time he was conceding sixteen to twenty pounds to his rivals, the equivalent of an eight- to ten-length head start. All Hands broke first, shooting to the lead, with Polylad a length behind. This time, Kelso moved with them, stalking the front runners just off the pace. With a half mile to go, Arcaro gunned his mount forward, accelerating with such speed he was in front by a length with three-eighths remaining. "It appeared at this point that it would be just a question of by how far he would go on to win."[10]

It appeared that way to Arcaro as well.[11] He eased his drive and moved to the rail, eager to let the field close, and save a slim victory for the finish. With a nineteen-pound advantage, jockey Pete Anderson on Our Hope had plans of his own. Driving Our Hope hard on the outside, he collared Kelso at the top of the stretch, and began to go by. "The crowd . . . was stunned."[12] But Kelso battled back, matching strides with his daring rival.

A hundred yards later, Our Hope lugged in, crowding Kelso, bumping him twice into the rail, securing a thin lead. Again, Kelso came back, wedged in so tightly there was no hope of getting past. As they plunged under the wire, it was Our Hope by a head. With a bent stirrup and white paint on his boot, Arcaro wasted no time in claiming foul. The judges reviewed the films, and there was no denying the charge: Kelso had been impeded twice in the stretch. Our Hope's number came down, and Kelso was awarded the race. Victory had been close, and far from decisive. Many believed Kelso had "hung" (failed to sustain his move) under the weight, and despite the bumping Our Hope would have prevailed. Mike Casale of *The Thoroughbred Record* disagreed: "I say Kelso, weight and all, would have beaten Our Hope had he not been knocked off stride in that crucial run to the wire. But he would not have beaten Our Hope by much." There seemed no reason for Tommy Trotter to penalize Kelso further in the upcoming Suburban Handicap.

Trotter, however, wasn't convinced. He'd seen the power of Kelso's early move and believed, as few did, the race might have ended there had Arcaro let him run when he could. If nothing else, Kelso was a tough nut to crack, and the longer distance of the Suburban should prove to his advantage. If Kelso wanted to chase the crown, he'd have to do it the hard way—as history intended—as Whisk Broom and Tom Fool had done before.

In 1908, anti-betting legislation caused all but twenty-five American tracks to close, forcing owners, riders, and horses, including Whisk Broom II, to seek their fortunes in England. In 1913, when racing returned to New York, Whisk Broom returned with it, appearing three times in the United States,[13] racing his way to handicap glory and induction in America's Hall of Fame. On Memorial Day, the six-year-old closed ten lengths to capture the Metropolitan Mile. Three weeks later, he returned, seizing the Brooklyn Handicap under 130 pounds in track record time. In the third and final jewel,[14] he packed a staggering 139 pounds to Triple Crown victory in an unbelievable two minutes flat—a new track and American record for the mile-and-a-quarter distance. Races were hand timed back then, and though eight other watches disputed the clocker's, the official time stood. By 1961, few believed it had ever happened, or on the Belmont surface, ever could. Whatever his time that day, Whisk Broom's Triple Crown achievement was unprecedented, and remained so for forty years.

In 1953, Tom Fool repeated the feat, running into history with ten victories in ten starts, including the prized handicap crown. Public attention focused on Native Dancer, and his quest for racing's more celebrated Crown. When Horse of the Year honors were announced, few realized the distinction went to Tom Fool. Seven years later, the National Turf Writers Association named the little-known colt "Horse of the Decade." Such was the scale of his achievement.

When weights were posted for the 1961 mile-and-a-quarter Suburban Handicap, Kelso was assigned 133 pounds. Only three horses had packed so much weight to Suburban victory, and those three were legends: Whisk Broom II, Grey Lag, and Bold Ruler. Like Kelso, Tom Fool had shouldered 130 pounds in the Met, but for the longer Suburban, he was dropped down to 128. Whisk Broom had carried 126 in the first leg and 130 in the second. Tom Trotter simply called it as he saw it. The ball was in Bohemia's court. In the end, Mrs. duPont decided. She accepted the challenge; her charge would run. It now fell to Hanford, Arcaro, and Kelso himself to deliver, or fail nobly trying.

With a ten- to twenty-three-pound pull in the weights, nine horses went forward to contest the champion. Sarcastic, the lone filly, burst to the front, closely followed by Francis S., Talent Show, and Kelso. Clear of the trouble that had plagued him in previous outings, "Kelso had dead aim on the leaders . . . almost from the outset."[15] At the half-mile pole, Arcaro made his move, sweeping "past the leaders as though they were standing still."[16] From there, it was a triumphant march to the finish, as Kelso opened daylight with each cadenced stride. Eased through the final sixteenth, he galloped under the wire with five lengths to spare, just four-fifths of a second off Sword Dancer's track record. Arcaro confided to Hanford: "That horse could have won off by himself."[17] To reporters, he said: "He's a monster."[18] Asked to compare him with other great horses he'd ridden, Arcaro hedged: "He's about as good as you'll ever see. . . . I will say I never rode a horse that was so powerful. He is the type that could handle those foreign horses."[19] It was the gelding's tenth straight victory. In the pages of the *Thoroughbred Record*, Mike Casale recorded the stunning victory:

> Kelso, one of the outstanding geldings of all time on
> the American turf, attained greater heights. . . on

Independence Day when, with the steadying impost of 133 pounds, he literally walked his beat in the 75th Suburban, oldest and most famous handicap in the land.

Amid tumultuous applause, this durable four-year-old . . . who definitely belongs in the same class with such other renowned geldings of the past as Exterminator and Armed, was under double wraps by Eddie Arcaro as he scored by five lengths at the end of the one-sided 1 1/4-mile contest. It was his easiest triumph, his most impressive.[20]

In truth, it wasn't supposed to be so easy. Tom Trotter would be honor-bound to increase his weight for the Brooklyn Handicap, third and final leg of the Crown. No doubt, the responsibility weighed heavily, and Trotter turned to the pages of history.[21] Tom Fool had carried 136 pounds to seal his Triple Crown. Discovery had packed the same weight to victory in 1936. Since 1887, no horse before or since has carried more. Kelso would be given the chance to duplicate Tom Fool's performance, if his connections accepted the challenge. In truth, the stable was relieved. Following his runaway Suburban, Hanford had feared as much as 140 pounds. Whatever doubts he had, he kept them to himself. Kelso would run.

The mile-and-a-quarter Brooklyn Handicap would prove one of the toughest trials of his career. On July 22, the temperature in New York soared to an oppressive 100 degrees as the field of ten marched to the post. On hand were Yorky, winner of the Widener Handicap, former rivals Don Poggio and Our Hope, and the rapidly improving Divine Comedy. Despite their strength, Kelso conceded twelve to thirty pounds to the group; nine to twenty-two lengths in the sweltering metropolitan heat.

When the gates opened, Divine Comedy exploded "as if powered by jet propulsion,"[22] building a six-length lead in the opening quarter. Behind him was lightly weighted Francis S., with Kelso third—twelve lengths behind the leader. In the backstretch, the margin grew to sixteen! Between the heat and weight, there was little Arcaro could do. It would be suicide to punish his horse in a vain attempt to chase the pace. With a half-mile remaining, Kelso was still third—Divine Comedy soaring twelve lengths ahead. From the stands, Tommy Trotter watched with concern. Perhaps he'd been wrong about the slender gelding. Divine Comedy was running too easily, and the tight finish he'd envisioned seemed hopelessly out of reach.[23]

On the far turn, Arcaro swung into action, thrusting his weight forward, pushing, prodding, urging his mount to greater speed. Kelso responded mightily, straining to catch the fleeing leaders. By the quarter-pole, he'd pared the margin to five and a half lengths.

Swinging outside on the final bend, Arcaro secured a straight course to the wire. He clucked to his mount and let the whip fall— once, twice, three times—again. The weight was taking its toll. The stretch seemed endless as Kelso strove desperately to close the gap. At the eighth pole, he collared Francis S., and drew within a length of Divine Comedy.

The whip fell again on the worn but willing warrior. Kelso replied with fury—bearing down on his remaining foe. Behind them, the pack stampeded. Divine Comedy clung to the lead; Kelso advanced relentlessly . . . Yorky bore down on Francis S. . . . Nine strides later, Kelso seized Divine Comedy, and with one mighty surge, plunged to a one-length lead. As the finish neared, he began to drift.

It was a weary horse that passed under the wire, a length and a quarter clear of the pack—a gallant and thoroughly spent Triple Crown Champion. Despite the heat and crushing burden, he had finished only two-fifths of a second off Sword Dancer's track mark. Carrying scale weight of ten pounds less, the record would have fallen.[24] William H. P. Robertson recorded: "[Kelso] had joined ... the most exclusive grouping of the American turf, winners of the Handicap Triple Crown,"[25] and as the historian depicted, he had done it best, carrying more cumulative weight in faster overall time then either of his worthy predecessors.

A breathless Arcaro returned to the scale. "I'll tell you one thing, that 136 pounds really tried him," he told reporters.[26] "Put 140 pounds on this horse, and you'll break him down. Hell, he had 139 when I got off. I checked it on the scale. The saddle cloth was dripping wet."[27]

Accolades poured in for the slender bay with legs of iron—and heart of gold. "Whatever question there happened to be concerning Kelso's status was effectively answered in the Brooklyn Handicap," read the tagline in *The Thoroughbred Record*:

> He's A Champion
>
> Kelso not only wrapped up the Horse-of-the-Year title for a second year in a row by carrying the crushing impost of 136 pounds to an electrifying triumph in the $100,000-added Brooklyn Handicap ... but the mighty gelding was being hailed, as well, as one of the all-time great performers of the century. . . . Driving relentlessly and strained to the last ounce of energy under the lash of Eddie's whipping, Kelso made a stretch charge of heroic dimension that carried him home winner by a length and a quarter. . . . It was a classic performance by a standout champion, one the greatest I have ever seen in some 40 years. They'll be talking about this 73rd running of the Brooklyn Handicap for years to come. Before Kelso came along to captivate turfdom with his dynam-

ic qualities as a racer, I'd always rated Tom Fool as the most outstanding four-year-old I'd ever seen in action. Now I don't know.[28]

Sports Illustrated offered the following: "As he ambles around the walking ring, Kelso hardly reveals the immense strength he possesses. But when he is in full flight in the stretch, his power is astonishing, and in the last yards of a race there is nothing running today that can equal him in courage."[29]

Eddie Arcaro, himself, would say later: "A number of good horses have won under 130 pounds, but every pound above that weight sits as heavy as 10 more on the average overnight horse. The difference between 130 and a greater weight is often the difference between a good horse and a great one. Kelso is a great horse."[30]

Following his tough race, Bohemia withdrew Kelso from the upcoming Man o' War Stakes, to give their champion a much-needed rest. On August 10, Mrs. duPont, Carl Hanford, and Eddie Arcaro were formally presented the *Morning Telegraph*'s 1960 Horse of the Year award. With half of 1961 behind, Charles Hatton reflected:

> In Mrs. duPont's ownership Kelso has gone on his winning way, uncomplainingly carrying weights that would stagger a mule. . . . Instead of placing an arbitrary 130 pound ceiling on the weight Kelso carries in handicaps, Mrs. duPont has accepted in good part the fundamental and very sporting philosophy that handicaps are designed to give all nominators the same winning chance. . . . She has set a shining example. . . . In a sense racing does itself honor in honoring Mrs. duPont.[31]

Eddie Arcaro spoke of Kelso: "I can't compare horses of different years, but I am sure of one thing and that is that I have never ridden a better horse than Kelso. Citation was a great horse but he was never asked to do the things that Kelso has done, weight carrying."[32]

Kelso moved to Chicago for the one-mile Washington Park Handicap on Labor Day. When race day dawned, Carl Hanford had cause for concern. The gelding was stepping gingerly, and it was too late to withdraw from the contest. Kelso had been shod a day earlier while stable hands rested, and the farrier didn't know his thin walled hooves wouldn't tolerate clipping. So in the normal course of trimming, he snipped, rather than filed, the gelding's tender feet. When Hanford arrived, he was furious. There was no recourse but to apply a thick layer of sealant[33] and send the champion into battle.

The track was hard and fast, as the field of eleven approached the gate. Kelso packed 132 pounds; twelve to twenty-seven pounds more than his competitors. It was trouble from the start. Ninth after the quarter, tenth after the half, Kelso was in distress, shaking his head and changing leads on the stinging surface. Nonetheless, he moved up to fourth, "and made a mild rally through the stretch run while showing a definite dislike for the going."[34] He was still fourth at the wire, six lengths behind the winner. His thirteen-month winning streak had come to an end. Bohemia offered no excuse. Carl Hanford told reporters, "I don't think the weight helped him any, but that is not our excuse. He was beaten."[35] Arcaro said simply, "He wasn't operating like he normally does, but he was beaten squarely. As far as carrying 132 pounds, when you run in a handicap race, you have to expect weight."[36] It was his first loss in eleven starts aboard the champion. From that day forward, Kelso would be shod infrequently, becoming one of the few horses in history to win back-to-back stakes in the same pair of shoes.[37]

Undaunted, Bohemia returned east for the fall weight-for-age classics, the Woodward Stakes and Jockey Club Gold Cup. All year, Kelso had competed under handicap conditions, toting high weight, conceding pounds and lengths to his rivals. Finally, in a fair contest, he would be at the mercy of none but his own limitations.

Under weight-for-age conditions, all horses of the same age carry the same weight. Three-year-olds carry four to six pounds less, depending on the time of year and distance. Fillies and mares receive an additional three-pound allowance. "In only eight years, the Woodward Stakes [had] become the most testing event in the U.S. racing calendar."[38] Contested at the classic American standard of a mile and a quarter on a dirt track, the race often matched Horse of the Year contenders for the first time. 1961 was no exception.

Kelso had faced full fields all year—eight, nine, ten opponents willing to challenge the champion so long as he was weighted down. When the lead came off, it was a different story. At even weights, only four horses dared contest him. All were worthy rivals. Topping the list was Carry Back, the sentimental favorite and undisputed three-year-old champion. Recovered from his Belmont injury, he had returned to form, crushing rivals in the Jerome Handicap. Divine Comedy was back for a second try, having advanced from the Brooklyn to defeat Tompion and Whodunit in the Saratoga Handicap. The latter two were fresh off a one-two punch in the mile-and-an-eighth Aqueduct Handicap, only a fifth of a second removed from the track record. On paper, it had all the ingredients of a horse race.

Kelso broke first, and was taken back, letting Divine Comedy set the pace, closely followed by Tompion. Unfettered by weight, Kelso went with them, tucked neatly on the rail two lengths off the leader. The pace was scalding, and after only five furlongs, Tompion crumbled. Kelso, well in hand, stalked the leader. Inside the half-pole, Arcaro launched his move.

Heads apart, the flying horses ran the mile in 1:34 4/5—equalling Count Fleet's twenty-year-old track record. And Kelso was only starting to roll. "It was fascinating to behold, as Kelso made it three, then four, five, six and seven, and finally eight lengths."[39] The gelding "was pricking his ears and beginning to loaf" as his margin grew.[40] Arcaro waved his stick and tapped his shoulder.

With complete authority, Kelso breezed under the wire eight lengths ahead of Divine Comedy. Carry Back was third, a half length farther back, with Whodunit another neck behind. There was a gasp from the crowd as the time was posted—2:00—two-minutes flat—at Belmont Park. It barely seemed possible. For the first time in forty-eight years, Whisk Broom's improbable record had been equaled. And this time, there was no disputing the clock. Kelso had achieved a milestone, and done so with speed to spare. He was now, quite simply, in a class of his own. As recorded by *The Thoroughbred Record*:

> In a true test, not confused by weight concessions, Kelso stood up to be measured.
>
> HE LOOKED GREAT
>
> In as extraordinary a performance as New Yorkers were ever privileged to see, spellbinding in its sheer magic output of power and speed, Mrs. Richard C. duPont's superlative racing machine equaled a track record of long standing in winning by eight lengths the eighth running of the Woodward Stakes . . .
>
> Amid the wild cheering of the excited crowd . . . Kelso tore the race apart in the final quarter-mile, leaving four worthy rivals, including Mrs. Katherine Price's gallant little Kentucky Derby-Preakness winner, Carry Back, outclassed beyond question. As he swooshed rhythmically and smoothly across the wire in this one-sided contest, the four-year old gelding by Your Host–Maid of Flight, by Count Fleet, was teletimed in 2:00 flat. This

matched the disputed track record set by Harry Payne Whitney's Whisk Broom II in the 1913 Suburban. . . . It's almost a certainty that Kelso would have broken the longstanding record if he had been forced to his full speed.[41]

His rider minced no praise: "I'm not kidding. I think he may be as great as Citation. Citation was the best I ever saw or rode, and since his day I've either ridden or ridden against every other good horse in the country. If Kelso goes on winning like this I'll have to say he's as good as Citation—and I never thought I'd be saying that about any other horse."[42]

Whitney Tower called it "one of the most remarkable races ever run in New York. . . . Kelso undoubtedly could have broken two minutes if Arcaro had realized that a record was in sight."[43] Tower continued:

> Ironically, for much the same reason that Tom Fool did not receive the full acclaim he deserved, Kelso has not been entirely accepted by the public. . . . A Kentucky Derby, Preakness, or Belmont winner wins fame automatically. What horses do when they become "old," at 4, is too often thought to be of no consequence. Since neither Tom Fool nor Kelso ran in any of the Triple Crown classics for 3-year-olds their accomplishments may never be fully appreciated.[44]

Nonetheless, experts like Charles Hatton knew what they had witnessed: "At this little moment in American turf history the lithe brown gelding stood upon a pedestal. Veterans were hard put to recall a more satisfying performance."[45]

With Horse of the Year honors sealed, and few worlds left to conquer, Kelso sallied forth for a second Jockey Club Gold Cup, attempting to become only the fifth horse in history to win the prestigious event two times.

Mad Hatter captured the first two-mile test in 1921, duplicating his performance the following year. Dark Secret triumphed in 1933, and prevailed in his final start as the "gallant and tragic figure"[46] of 1934. Driving through a sea of mud, he fractured a foreleg in the Gold Cup stretch. "But with the fracture widening, and Faireno driving beside him, Dark Secret lasted incredibly to win by a head."[47] His foreleg shattered, the colt was destroyed, but decades later, his legend endures.

Firethorn, second to Omaha in the Preakness and Belmont Stakes, captured both the 1935 and 1937 renditions, "reveling in the two-mile distance."[48] In 1955, burly Nashua capped Horse of the Year honors with his first score, and returned a year later to set a new track and American record for the distance.

In 1961, only three outclassed rivals were found to test Kelso at the grueling distance. By post time, his odds were 1–10, despite cancellation of place and show betting.

Kelso broke fast but was immediately hauled in, allowing Diehard II of Argentina to assume command. Behind him, Kelso was "crying to run,"[49] mouth wide open against his rider's choking grip. Arcaro straightened his legs and thrust them forward, applying the weight of his body against the reins. Kelso pulled harder. Past the stands for the first time, Arcaro began "swinging his mount"[50]—literally—to avoid overrunning the leader. With three-quarters of a mile remaining, he could hold the gelding no longer. Entering the backstretch, they sailed past the leader. In front, with Arcaro lifted high in the saddle, Kelso began to relax.

On he bobbed down the backstretch and into the curve, with the field stretched five lengths behind. On the far turn,

Hillsborough launched a furious drive, closing the gap to three lengths as they rounded the bend for home. Arcaro eased his grip. It was Kelso by four at the head of the stretch, and it was Kelso by five at the wire, galloping with ears pricked the length of the straightaway, a radiant two-time Gold Cup winner. The marathon had been little more than a workout—a long, slow, afternoon ride that failed to break a sweat. The gelding wasn't even blowing hard.

"The Cup was about as easy as a horse can win,"[51] Arcaro told reporters. "He could have done 15 lengths better this year than last if he had to. . . . Kelso is one of the greatest—if not the greatest— horses I have ever ridden."[52] *The Thoroughbred Record* called it: "one of the most one-sided stakes events on record."[53] *The Blood-Horse* chimed: "The time of the race, 3:25 4/5, has no meaning because he was under a pull the whole way. The margin was five lengths, but it could have been twenty."[54] Charles Hatton of the *Daily Racing Form* concluded: "The whole affair looked ludicrous. . . . This observer saw Count Fleet win the Belmont by roughly 100 lengths,[55] and Top Flight trot past the finish of an Acorn, but it is inconceivable any horse more completely outclassed his rivals than Kelso did in his second Jockey Club Gold Cup success."[56]

By now, Americans journalists were touting Kelso as the best racehorse in the world. Only a triumph in the Washington, D.C. International at Laurel, Prix de l'Arc de Triomphe at Longchamp,[57] or King George VI and Queen Elizabeth Stakes at Ascot could confirm the claim. Kelso was invited for the second year to participate in the International, and this time Mrs. duPont accepted.

In 1961, the International was a prestigious invitational event, pitting the finest horses on the globe willing to tackle the journey. Run under classic European conditions—one and a half miles on a grass course—horses started from behind a Newmarket barrier—a strung net, lifted when horses approached the tape in order of proper post position. For all but turf specialists, grass was a foreign surface for American horses, one on which they weren't conditioned to compete.[58] It would be Kelso's maiden voyage on a turf course,[59] and his first "walk-up" start. Hanford was confident he could handle both. So were reporters, and Kelso appeared on the cover of *Sports Illustrated*: "America's Kelso Against Them All."[60]

Since 1953, only two American horses had captured the international event: Fisherman in 1954 and Bald Eagle, twice, in 1959 and 1960. Other renditions had been claimed by France (three times), England, Argentina, and Australia. In 1961, the United States would be represented by Kelso and T.V. Lark. "T.V. Lark's grass-running ability and current good form made him a particularly apt selection."[61] With Arcaro on Kelso, and veteran John Longden on T.V. Lark, the Americans stood to deliver a one-two punch. Zabeg of Russia, Misti of France, and Prenupcial of Venezuela formed the principal threats. Wonderboy of Denmark, Irtysch of Russia, and the Irish filly Sail Cheoil were accorded little chance.

The horses and riders approached the tape. Arranged in proper order, starter Eddie Blind wasted no time. The tape lifted and the field was off. Only Sail Cheoil, beside Kelso, broke behind the field.[62]

Kelso shot to the front from the outside, as T.V. Lark secured second on the rail. They were one-two sailing into the clubhouse turn, and one-two after a half, with Kelso reeling off record-breaking fractions, a half-length ahead of his American rival.

On the backstretch, the two maintained their positions—Kelso on top, T.V. Lark lapped and stalking. After five furlongs, Arcaro pulled clear and crossed to the rail. A length now separated the American runners. With one mile down, and a half-mile remaining, John Longden launched his drive. Arcaro glanced back. The

American horse was no threat, and he focused on the European chargers behind. What he saw was heartening; the foreigners were strung ten lengths to the rear.

On the far turn, T.V. Lark loomed on the outside. Arcaro sat down to ride. It was time to stamp Kelso's mark on the world. T.V. Lark moved with him.

In an instant, Arcaro realized his mistake. He had underestimated the American colt. Despite the scalding pace, T.V. Lark was far from finished, and ready to launch his own bid for glory.

Together they drove through the final turn—T.V. Lark glued to the gelding's side, Kelso straining to put him away. Circling the bend, Kelso overreached his stride, swerving as he struck an ankle.[63] Bearing down on his good leg, he wrenched that one as well.[64] Oblivious to the pain, he battled on.

Head and head, compatriots dueled for the wire. This was not the finale Arcaro envisioned. At the eighth-pole, T.V. Lark thrust his head in front. Kelso waged back, but T.V. Lark wedged out— sweeping under the wire three-quarters of a length on top— smashing the track record by one and four-fifth seconds. Kelso was a fifth of a second behind.

Arcaro was an angry rider when he vaulted from the saddle, angry with himself for failing his mount. "If they'd run this race tomorrow, we'd win. I'd know what to do, and we'd win,"[65] he said. T.V. Lark was draped in laurel, while John Longden basked in well-deserved glory. In the jockeys' room, Arcaro recovered his grace: "I thought I could put T.V. Lark away any time I wanted to. . . . I thought I had him under control. I wanted to open up a lead at the quarter pole, but when I couldn't shake Longden then I knew I had my hands full. Kelso handled the grass perfectly and he ran his race. We just ran into a tiger and got beat."[66]

Kelso cooled out well, and when Hanford arrived at the barn the following morning, he was shocked by what he found. Kelso's right hock, the critical midpoint of his rear leg,[67] was swollen, literally to the size of a football. Moments later, Doc Pace, the state veterinarian, appeared:

"How's his leg this morning, Carl?"

"How'd you know about that?" Hanford replied.

"I was there at the start when it happened. That filly [Sail Cheoil] kicked him so hard, it sounded like a cannon going off."[68]

Kelso had blistered the entire mile and a half with a severe blow to his rear leg. Further examination revealed heat and swelling in both front ankles. Likely, he had suffered one sprain, then the other, straining to compensate for his injured hock. It was left for the press to speculate. Carl Hanford would only say, "We're not offering the injuries as an alibi for Kelso's loss. Kelso ran a terrific race, and so did T.V. Lark, only T.V. Lark ran better."[69]

In retrospect, "T.V. Lark did himself proud,"[70] running the most brilliant race of his career, shattering the course record, and defeating one of the sport's great legends in his prime. He more then earned his title: Best Grass Horse of the Year.

For his part, Kelso was a hero in defeat. "It is to Kelso's credit," Charles Hatton asserted, "that . . . injuring himself for and aft . . . he fought back with leonine courage all through the stretch."[71] The injuries were not alibis; they were confirmation. Finishing on one sound leg, he had met the ultimate test head on and hadn't faltered. A great horse needs no excuse.

The International did nothing to dim Kelso's luster. "At season's end," wrote Charles Hatton, "every disciple . . . from Laurel to Longchamp, and behind the Iron Curtain to Moscow, knew that in Kelso a great horse passed their way."[72] Once again, Kelso was voted Horse of the Year, the third horse in history to achieve that honor twice. Had the young gelding never raced again, his place in history would have been secure.

Kelso and Carry Back running neck and neck as they turn for home in the 1962 Washington, D.C. International. (Laurel Race Course)

Chapter Five

A Hero in Defeat

ONTINUE TO RACE ANY HORSE in handicaps, in the most exclusive circles and under the severest penalties, and he is bound to lose his share. Kelso was no exception.

Following his Laurel injuries, Kelso returned to Woodstock Farm. By day, he romped with blue-blood companions; at dusk he grazed with deer. His ankles healed quickly, but a month passed before his rear leg could withstand training. In January 1962, he was again shipped to the Aiken Training Center in South Carolina. In March, Eddie Arcaro announced his retirement from racing, believing it unfair to continue competing simply to ride the champion. In April, demonstrations erupted against the arrest of seven Freedom Riders in Georgia. Seven hundred protesters, including the Reverend Martin Luther King, Jr., were arrested and jailed. That same month, Kelso contracted a virus, forcing him out of training, and delaying his return to the track. Faced with the prospect of finding a new rider, Hanford consulted Arcaro. "Shoemaker," came the reply, a jockey with a record to match his own.

In May, five-year-old Kelso arrived at Belmont Park, in pursuit of a second Handicap Crown. Gone was the gaunt horse of youth. In his place stood a sleek, slender thoroughbred, with sculpted head, dappled hide, and massive hindquarters, built for "power and drive."[1] Overall, Charles Hatton described: "Kelso's head is his most appealing point, esthetically, though any horseman would be quick to note the extraordinary propulsive power across his loins, and wide hips. These recall a souped-up Ford, with Cadillac horsepower, and are almost an abnormality."[2] His handsome head he portrayed as a "model of quality"[3]—reminiscent of Hyperion— with delicate muzzle, fine-tapered ears, and "large, luminous"[4] eyes, brimming with intelligence and character.

Six and a half months had elapsed since his Laurel defeat, and the gelding was in need of a "sharpener"—a short race to hone his speed for the Metropolitan Mile. Try as he might, Carl Hanford was thwarted. Each time Kelso's name appeared in the entries, the race failed to fill. No one, it seemed, wanted any part of the champion. On May 19, Kelso appeared for a seven-furlong workout between races at Aqueduct. He was joined by Cyane, a Belmont eligible seeking a similar spot. For three quarters of a mile, they ran together. In the final furlong, Kelso bounded away by five lengths, scalding seven furlongs in the track record time of 1:22, and pulling up a mile in 1:35 "with Willie Shoemaker standing as straight in the irons as a cigar-store Indian."[5]

That was all Tom Trotter needed to see. Despite his long layoff, Kelso was assigned 133 pounds for the Metropolitan Mile—three pounds more than he had carried the year before, and ten to twenty-five pounds more than the rest of the field. Expectations were high for the partnership with Shoemaker, but one factor seemed overlooked—the size of his new rider. At only ninety-eight pounds,[6] the talented "Shoe" weighed twelve pounds less than Arcaro. Almost thirty-five pounds of lead would be required to achieve his assigned load. Lacking a bona-fide race, Kelso was forced into the contest cold—with the weight, quite literally, stacked against him. The field was formidable.

Carry Back had returned at four, faster and stronger than ever. And he was well seasoned from a vigorous winter campaign. Assigned 123 pounds for the Metropolitan, he would be receiving a ten-pound advantage from Kelso. "If Carry Back is ever to beat Kelso, this is it," trainer Jack Price asserted.[7]

Kelso broke well, and was eased to sixth, while Carry Back raced just three lengths behind. Twelve lengths ahead, Hitting Away and Rullah Red dueled at a suicidal pace. Together, they reached six furlongs in 1:08 flat. It was inevitable they would collapse, and they did. On the backstretch, Carry Back moved to the gelding on the outside. For a quarter of a mile, Kelso kept pace. Carry Back was striding smoothly; Kelso was laboring. Running full tilt down the straightaway, Carry Back passed Kelso and swept by the leaders at the eighth pole, drawing off by two and a half lengths in track record time. His clocking equaled that of Bald Eagle in 1960, and a little-known colt, Beau Purple, just weeks earlier. Kelso "raced evenly to the stretch, but failed to respond when set down for the drive,"[8] finishing sixth, eight lengths behind the winner. After two years and twelve races, it was the first time Kelso had lost a race in New York. The *Times* related the story:

> Carry Back Ties Aqueduct Mark in Winning Metropolitan
> 63,065 SEE KELSO RUN SIXTH AT 3-5
> Carry Back, in 1:33.6 Mile, Tops Million in Earnings
>
> Carry Back ran the greatest race of his career yesterday in winning the Metropolitan Mile at Aqueduct. Mrs. Katherine Price's colt, who gained national fame and popularity by his thrilling finishes in the Kentucky Derby and Preakness last year, exceeded himself in capturing the sixty-ninth running of the handicap.... Carry Back came from "way back," according to his custom, to register his smashing success.

As for Kelso, the gelding "showed no inclination to run, even with Willie Shoemaker to urge him. The Bohemia gelding, now a five-year-old, was no threat at any time, and finished sixth."[9]

Shoemaker said simply: "No excuses at all. That 133 pounds and his idleness made the difference."[10] Hanford told reporters: "Our future plans remain unchanged. We'll go in the Suburban and Brooklyn. As for the Met, it was just a question of too much lead."[11]

Still seeking a soft spot, Hanford entered his charge two weeks later in the mile-and-an-eighth Nassau County Handicap. Kelso was assigned 132 pounds, and that alone posed a dilemma. Likely it wouldn't stop him in the Nassau County, but victory at that weight could result in a crushing impost for the Suburban, against far tougher competition. At the last minute, fate intervened. Scanning the condition books, Hanford spotted a minor contest for non-winners of a race since October. Kelso qualified. Quietly, Hanford dropped Kelso's name in the box. The event filled, and under conditions specified by the race, Kelso snuck in with 117 pounds. Also entered was the consistent and hard-hitting Garwol, a stakes-caliber colt himself. Hastily, track officials renamed the event the Clem McCarthy Memorial, lest a horse of Kelso's caliber win a race dubbed the "Shuffle-Along."

Kelso "broke alertly"[12] and settled into fourth, never more than two lengths behind Garwol's pace. Approaching the far turn, he improved his position to second, still two lengths removed from the leader. Then he began to roll. At the eighth pole, he collared the frontrunner. "Moving smoothly and with graceful strides that seemed to belie his speed,"[13] Kelso flashed under the wire two lengths ahead of Garwol, but he wasn't through running. The gelding continued past the finish line, "going out"[14] a mile and an eighth in 1:48 1/5, a full second faster than Beau Prince's run in the

Nassau County, and at a mile and a quarter, eased up, in 2:03 flat, despite the lack of competition. It was a convincing display. That afternoon, Beau Prince won the feature, but the lead line was Kelso's: "Kelso Scores at Belmont; Beau Prince Wins Stakes." Tommy Trotter was impressed, and said so: "That race showed that he's back to last year's form."[15]

On July 4th, Kelso and Carry Back appeared for a rematch in the seventy-sixth running of the Suburban Handicap. Only two horses accepted the challenge: Garwol, and the front-running speedball, Beau Purple. Neither was accorded a chance, not against the big guns, and certainly not at a mile and a quarter. Toting 132 pounds, Kelso conceded four pounds to Carry Back, 17 to Beau Purple, and 23 pounds to Garwol. Despite high weight, Kelso again went off as the favorite.

As expected, Beau Purple surged to the front. Garwol ran closest, three lengths behind, with Kelso on the rail three lengths farther back. Carry Back was last, but in close contention, only six and a half lengths off the pace. All were stalking, poised for the moment when Beau Purple would fold. Kelso was the first to move. With three-quarters down, and a half-mile to go, he swept past Garwol and moved into second place, perfectly positioned two lengths off the frontrunner. With three-eighths of a mile remaining, Shoemaker launched his winning drive. So it appeared. Not to Bill Boland on Beau Purple. Fresh and full of run as they rounded the final turn, the speedy colt unleashed a blistering final quarter in 24 seconds. In the end, the story was his:

> Beau Purple Outruns Kelso and Carry Back in $105,200 Suburban Handicap
> Aqueduct Victor Sets Track Mark
> Beau Purple Runs 1 1/4 Miles in 2:00 3/5—Kelso, Garwol and Carry Back Follow[16]

Kelso ran determinedly, but never gained, as Beau Purple swept under the wire with two and a half lengths to spare, four-fifths of a second faster than Sword Dancer's track record! The "sprinter" had gone the distance, and done so with surprising class. Garwol hung on for third, a length in front of Carry Back. It was Beau Purple's third record of the season. "Boland stole the Suburban on Beau Purple, one of the fastest thoroughbreds in recent years," recorded *The Thoroughbred Record*. "That his reputation as a speed horse is genuine, is best indicated by the fact that he had already set one track record (1:21 4/5 for seven furlongs at Hialeah) and equaled another (1:33 3/5 for a mile at Aqueduct) earlier this year."[17]

As for Kelso, the journal noted: "Kelso, a year older and perhaps not as good as he was in 1961, did spot Beau Purple 17 pounds, quite a concession. . . . The weight unquestionably told on Kelso."[18] No doubt. At a mile and a quarter, seventeen pounds was equal to a twelve-length headstart. Kelso lost by two and a half. As Arcaro had predicted a year earlier: "He has to get beat sometime if he keeps on running in the handicaps, but it won't be because he isn't the better horse."[19]

With the first two events split between Carry Back and Beau Purple, 1962 would see no Handicap Crown winner. An unknown sprinter had tossed his hat in the ring, Carry Back was stronger than ever, and Kelso, under high weight, open to defeat. As time progressed, the battle for Horse of the Year honors grew more confused.

Ten days later, Kelso, Carry Back, and Beau Purple squared off in the mile-and-a-quarter Monmouth Park Handicap, the first of three events billed that season as "race of the year." Also entered were Garwol, Polylad, and Hitting Away. Kelso was assigned 130 pounds, Carry Back 124, and Beau Purple 117. In effect, Kelso was conceding four to nine lengths to his rivals.

Hitting Away was out first, but it was Garwol, not Beau Purple, that ran with him. By the clubhouse turn, Hitting Away had opened a length on Garwol, with Beau Purple tucked in third, two lengths behind. Kelso was fourth, Carry Back sixth. In the backstretch, Beau Purple swept by Garwol, just one length behind Hitting Away. Hitting Away and Beau Purple hit the far turn on top. Kelso and Carry Back ran heads apart, three lengths back.

Rounding the stretch, the artillery fired. Beau Purple passed Hitting Away. Carry Back circled wide on the outside. Kelso moved on the rail. Down the straightaway they charged. Carry Back passed Beau Purple in mid-stretch and drew out. Kelso, on the inside, passed the tenacious horse next. Both Polylad and Garwol passed Hitting Away. In the end, Carry Back swept under the wire three lengths ahead of Kelso, with Beau Purple another three-quarters of a length behind. Polylad was fourth; Garwol fifth. "Hitting Away was last after taking them all on one by one. He ran a courageous race."[20]

The headline belonged to Carry Back:

CARRY BACK OUTRUNS KELSO
Winner of Rich Monmouth Sets Mark with Late Rush.[21]

In short, Carry Back was sensational. He exceeded even his Metropolitan victory, smashing Round Table's fifteen-year-old track record by four-fifths of a second! "Carry Back . . . came by the stands the first time last. He came by the stands the last time first. That was all there was to it."[22]

A week later, Carry Back and Beau Purple contested the Brooklyn Handicap, third jewel in the Handicap Crown. Beau Purple "got the jump on the speed horses . . . and drew out to win by 3 1/2 lengths"[23] in two minutes flat on the Aqueduct surface, smashing his own track record by three-fifths of a second. Carry

Back was fourth, conceding eleven pounds to the victor. The two longest races in the handicap series had fallen to Beau Purple. The "sprinter," it appeared, could sprint any distance.

Kelso had stayed in the barn. Two weeks behind schedule when the season started, Hanford needed more time to hone the gelding's edge. At Saratoga in early August, Kelso suffered a second illness, pushing his schedule back even further.

That left the August 4 Whitney Stakes to Carry Back. Carrying 130 pounds for the first time, he scored impressively, conceding nineteen pounds to his old rival, Crozier, and beating him decisively by two lengths. That race, more than any other, confirmed what many already believed: Carry Back at four was a far better horse than the three-year-old champion who had squeaked by Crozier in duel after memorable duel.

While Kelso recovered, Shoemaker returned to California. Shortly after, he relinquished his mount on Kelso to race in Chicago, and the search for a new rider began. This time, Hanford chose Ismael (Milo) Valenzuela, a heavier, more powerful rider than Shoemaker, seemingly tailor-made for the headstrong, top-weighted runner "who liked to be held together."[24] Known for his forceful finishes and ability to switch hands "like a magician,"[25] Valenzuela was the best Indian wrestler in the jockeys' room, both arm-to-arm, and with the middle digit of his hand. The strong horse needed a strong rider. He got one in spades.

On August 22, Kelso went to the post for the first time at Saratoga, and his first appearance under the guidance of Milo Valenzuela. It would prove a partnership that glowed as richly as that of Kelso and Arcaro.

The event was a minor allowance race, contested at a mile and a sixteenth on the turf course. Kelso, carrying 124 pounds, stalked from fourth place in the field of seven, moved up on the far turn, and assumed a half-length lead at the head of the stretch. He drew off to win "ridden out"[26] by one and a half lengths over the fast-closing Call the Witness. His time was three-fifths of a second off the course record. Reporters expected more. Charles Hatton, Kelso's greatest admirer in 1961, described the champion as "a pallid shadow of his former self . . . more like a crumbling idol than a bidder for Horse-of-the-Year honors."[27]

When racing returned to Aqueduct, Carry Back and Beau Purple locked horns again, this time in a one-mile overnight contest. Carrying 133 pounds, Carry Back abandoned his late-running style to race Beau Purple into early submission and win going away by eight lengths. Under 127 pounds, Beau Purple faded to last.

Kelso pursued a separate path. Training for Labor Day's Aqueduct Handicap, he punctured a hind ankle that became infected, forcing him out of training for the third time that year.[28] Milo was booked elsewhere on September 8, when Kelso resurfaced for a minor grass race at Atlantic City with Don Pierce aboard. Kelso dueled the long shot, Hy Prince, through the early stages. With a half-mile remaining, he swept to the front. In previous years, it would have ended there. On this day, the pack closed. "In a cavalry charge to the wire"[29] it was Call the Witness first; Art Market second. Kelso was a "dead short horse,"[30] and to many it appeared he was finished as a champion.

While critics judged, Carl Hanford sought a reason for his recent dull efforts. Suspecting the cold spring water of Saratoga had chilled his stomach, Kelso was given nothing but bottled water for over a week. His vitality returned.

On September 19, Valenzuela was up for the second time when Kelso emerged for the mile-and-a-quarter Stymie Handicap at Aqueduct. Spotting fourteen to twenty-two pounds to the field, Kelso stalked in third place behind Grey Eagle and Garwol. In the backstretch, he moved with a rush, opening a length and a half on the field as they turned for home. From there, he cruised, galloping under the wire two and a half lengths in front of Polylad. It was Thursday when the morning news brought results, and for the second time under Milo, the headline was Kelso's:

> Kelso Wins Stymie for His First Stakes Victory of Year
> FAVORITE SCORES IN 11-HORSE FIELD
>
> "The champ is back in form," was the essence of the crowd reaction at Aqueduct yesterday, after Mrs. Richard C. duPont's Kelso won the Stymie Handicap. . . . The archivists in the crowd of 26,111 could not forget that Kelso, now a 5-year-old, was the Horse of the Year for 1960 and 1961. He showed more than a semblance of that championship form in turning in a time figure of 2:00 4/5 in taking the Stymie, and he did it under the burden of 128 pounds.[31]

When Milo spoke to reporters, his words rang like those of Arcaro: "He ran real fine today. I just sat and waited the early part and when I asked him to run, he just pulled away. At the finish, he was running easy."[32] Hanford spoke with confidence, "This is the first time he's been right all season. We'll go in the Woodward next."[33] Even Charles Hatton was surprised:

> Kelso has come back. Ailing and pounds below his best form much of the season, Mrs. Richard C. duPont's gelding pulled up to his Stymie rivals a mile and a quarter in 2:00 4/5 under 128 pounds. This was by way of announcing his candidacy for Horse of the Year honors a third time.
>
> Kelso followed Grey Eagle like a shadow to the last bend, strolled to the front at Milo's pleasure and finished with his rider's feet over the dash.[34]

Veteran timers contended he would have bettered two minutes, had Milo lifted his feet from the brakes.[35] I held my breath, lest the magic fade. And like an elixir, the bottle water continued for the remainder of Kelso's career.

On September 29, he appeared for the second straight year in the weight-for-age Woodward Stakes. Rivals Beau Purple and T.V. Lark were there, as was three-year-old champion Jaipur, winner of four straight, including the Belmont and Travers Stakes in a memorable duel with Ridan. The track was "good," not fast, and contenders were reshod with "mud calks" to handle the deep going. Hanford, fearing a repeat of Chicago, chose not to replace the gelding's plates. In the paddock, he appeared more confident and relaxed than he had all season. "Kelly's himself again," he beamed, "and when Kelly's himself they don't come much better."[36]

Beau Purple shot to the front as expected, opening eight lengths on the field by the head of the backstretch. Jaipur was second, two lengths in front of Kelso. They raced that way for three-quarters of a mile, with Beau Purple maintaining the comfortable lead and easy pace of a "race thief." Against this Kelso, it wasn't enough. When Kelso moved, "it was less of a move than a bolt,"[37] closing seven and a half lengths in a quarter of a mile, sweeping past Jaipur and Beau Purple as though they were standing still, and finishing the mile three lengths on top of the field. "In the stretch Kelso was striding so smoothly that it seemed a symphony of motion, and when Jaipur . . . game to the end, came at him once more, it took only a cluck or two, a dig of the knees, a brush with the whip, to urge him out to more daylight."[38]

Kelso swept under the wire four and half lengths on top, winning with his ears pricked, "as the rider pleased."[39] Jaipur easily outclassed the rest of the field, finishing six and a half lengths in front of Guadalcanal, with Hitting Away fourth and Beau Purple, fifth. It was Kelso's second Woodward victory, and his was the buzz.

Tearing up losing tickets on Jaipur, David Alexander concluded: "I concede without reservation after his effort in the Woodward. . . that Kelso is the best horse in this country, weight-for-age, which is, I suppose, saying in effect that weight-for-age gives you the only true measure of a real race horse. . . . Kelly was again proving that you can't take champions lightly when they have an even rattle and roll in the weights."[40]

Charles Hatton effused:

> Kelso did not just beat Jaipur, Beau Purple, T.V. Lark and the others in the Woodward. He humiliated them. In one fell swoop, like a hawk buzzing a barnyard of chickens, he made up easily 10 lengths going to the end of the backstretch, en route passing Jaipur and Beau Purple, then glided home by four and one half length in 2:03 1/5. The margin and time were merely rhetorical. . . . [Kelso] has undergone a striking metamorphosis in a few short weeks since he was "life and death" to beat a moderate field in a turf race at the Spa.[41]

A glowing Valenzuela told reporters: "That other horse, Beau Purple, got out so far that I moved earlier than I expected to. Then, when my horse got going, I just kept moving. I never hit him."[42] It was Milo's third victory in as many starts on the gelding, and he had yet to draw his whip.

The same reporters who had written Kelso off a month earlier now flocked to him. Hanford chided: "Where were you guys before the race. You were all knocking my horse saying he wasn't the same as last year. . . . How could anyone knock him when he was second in both those races with high weight and the races were run in record time? . . . I'm not concerned now about Horse of the Year. Our next objective is the Jockey Gold Cup October 20th at Belmont."[43]

In October, Carry Back boarded a plane for France, en route to the Prix de l'Arc de Triomphe at Longchamp. Beau Purple moved to Chicago for the Hawthorne Gold Cup, and Kelso remained in New York for the two-mile Jockey Club Gold Cup. In France, Carry Back finished tenth in a crowded twenty-four-horse field, only five and three-quarter lengths behind the long-shot winner, Soltikoff. His normally congenial trainer was openly critical of the ride he received from an indifferent jockey, and Carry Back returned to the United States.

On October 20, the Jockey Club Gold Cup returned to Belmont Park, scene of historic renditions, and Kelso was attempting to become the first horse to win the prestigious event three times. Nashua's American record had fallen to Kelso at Aqueduct in 1960, but his track record still stood when Kelso appeared at Belmont in 1962.

With Kelso also entered in the mile-and-a-half Man o' War Stakes only a week away, Hanford's instructions for the Gold Cup were simple: "win as easily as possible." The gates clanked open and the forty-third running of the Jockey Gold Cup was on. Tutankhamen, Kelso, and Troubador III ran bunched together for the first half-mile, with Tutankhamen setting the early tempo. Kelso, under a tight hold, was close behind. When Tutankhamen faded, Troubador moved up to secure the lead, and held it by half a length when they hit the mile pole. Kelso could be restrained no longer, and with a mile remaining, moved effortlessly past. Milo didn't move at all.

Down the backstretch and into far turn they galloped, two lengths ahead of the field. A mile and a half flashed past in 2:28 2/5, faster than all but three renditions of the Belmont Stakes.[44] By the far turn, even the strength of Milo couldn't hold him. For an eighth of a mile, Kelso ran with abandon, as his margin grew— two, four, five, then six, seven, eight lengths—as they rolled into the upper stretch. And the margin continued to grow—ten lengths, twelve lengths—as Kelso romped, ears pricked, down the long straightaway. He was ten lengths on top as he galloped under the wire. Victory was so effortless, his time unbelievable. As recorded by the *New York Times*:

> KELSO WINS BELMONT GOLD CUP THIRD TIME
> TRACK MARK SET
> Kelso Captures 2-Mile Race by 10 Lengths—
> Guadalcanal 2d
>
> Kelso demonstrated yesterday that he could go on to be the perennial horse of the year as long as his owner, Mrs. Richard C. duPont, might choose to run him. The 5-year-old gelded son of Your Host won the $108,900 Jockey Club Gold Cup at Belmont just about as easily as his rider, Ismael Valenzuela, wanted him to. He beat his nearest foe, Mrs. Robert Dotter's Guadalcanal, by 10 lengths, and, despite the ease of the conquest, covered the two miles in the track record time of 3 minutes 19 4/5 seconds.[45]

Kelso had toppled Nashua's track record, running the fastest two miles in fifty-six years of Belmont racing. And his achievement was unprecedented. In 3 minutes 19 4/5 seconds, Kelso became the only horse in history to capture the Gold Cup three times. "Kelso ran one of the best races of his career in the Jockey Club Gold Cup, winning for the third straight year and proving that he still is the best horse in America," wrote David Alexander for *The Blood-Horse*. "It was the quality of Kelso's race rather than the quality of the field that made it so impressive. . . . Kelso's move at the head of the stretch called up visions of Man o' War and Citation. . . . On the basis of the Gold Cup, I'm forced to think that Kelso is not only the greatest gelding since Exterminator, but the greatest racehorse America has seen since Citation."[46]

Milo said simply, "He won it real easy."[47] In truth, his arms were so sore he was forced to cancel the remainder of his mounts. Years later, Carl Hanford would recall: "Milo said he couldn't straighten his arms for two days, he had that much hold of the horse the whole time."[48] The strong horse needed a strong rider.

That same day, Beau Purple triumphed in Chicago, defeating Bass Clef by two lengths in the Hawthorne Gold Cup. It was his seventh victory in seventeen starts that year.

Two days later, on October 22, President Kennedy addressed the nation. U-2 reconnaissance had revealed Soviet missiles on the island of Cuba, just ninety miles from U.S. shores. President Kennedy announced a naval blockade of the island, concluding with a threat: any missile launched from Cuba would be considered an attack on the United States by the Soviet Union. The following day, naval vessels were in place. That same day, new reconnaissance revealed that Soviet missiles were poised for launch.

On October 24, Soviet ships steamed toward Cuba. Families with backyard fallout shelters, including my hometown mayor, made last-minute preparations. The eyes of the nation fixed on television, and a somber Walter Cronkite broadcasting from New York. On course and at full velocity, the Soviet ships steamed, visible on our screen, little more than a hundred yards from the line of quarantine drawn in Caribbean waters. Like a naval cavalry, they charged. . . . Suddenly, they slowed. Then just as suddenly, the stampeding engines stilled. At the last possible moment, radio orders from Moscow had told them to hold position.

The following day, U.S. Ambassador Adlai Stevenson confronted the Soviet Union at the United Nations. The Soviets refused to answer. American military forces were set at DEFCON-2, the highest alert in U.S. history.

As the chess match between war and peace continued, 33,000 dauntless fans flocked through the turnstiles to witness the Man o' War Stakes. On Saturday, October 27, twelve thoroughbreds answered the bugler's call to the post. It was a bittersweet unfolding, as though the band played while the Titanic went down. Global survival hung by a thread, but at venerable old Belmont, the ancient sport displayed its timeless pageantry, invincible to the winds of change.

Billed largely as a run-off between Carry Back and Kelso, in truth it was one of the finest fields ever assembled for one race on American soil. At a mile and a half on the grass, under weight-for-age conditions, it pitted the "big three"—Carry Back, Kelso, and Beau Purple—against grass course specialists Wise Ship, The Axe II, and T.V. Lark. Joining them were two of the finest French three-year-olds: the filly Monade and the colt Val de Loir. Between them, they had amassed the Epsom Oakes, Prix de Vermeille, French Derby, and Prix Hocquart, all at a mile and a half on the grass. Together, they had finished second and third to Soltikoff in the Prix de l'Arc de Triomphe. Both had to be schooled from the gate to compete.

Charles Hatton picked Kelso, Carry Back, and Monade, in that order. The writer, who a year before had said "a great horse never has an excuse," now wrote that Kelso would need to be "the greatest" to succeed, considering:

> (A) Never in history has any horse of top quality come from two miles to win a stake at a mile and a half within a week.

> (B) Never has one attempted to do so while moving from the main track to the grass.

> (C) Never does a horse run two miles in 3:19 4/5

without some expenditure of energy, it does not matter by how many lengths he beats the second to the finish.[49]

Hanford was confident, and his instructions to Milo were simple: "Watch The Axe and don't move too soon. Beau Purple and Carry Back won't go the distance."[50]

As expected, Beau Purple out broke the field. By the end of the first half-mile, he had one and a half lengths on Wise Ship and two and a half lengths on Monade. The long shot, Honey Dear, was third, a half-length back, with Kelso fourth, another half-length behind. The French filly was effectively boxed on the rail. Behind them, The Axe II and Carry Back ran sixth and seventh, each within striking range. With a mile down, the order had barely changed. Only three lengths separated the first five horses. Carry Back and The Axe held their positions. Time for the mile was 1:39 1/5.

Milo sensed it. The pace was slow, dangerously so. Nonetheless, he sat chilly as instructed with The Axe behind him. Then rapidly, things began to shift. In front, Beau Purple extended his lead to two lengths. He wasn't coming back to the field; he was accelerating. Kelso stalked in second. Honey Dear, Wise Ship, and Monade dropped back. The Axe II and Carry Back launched their drives.

On the lead, at his own tempo, Beau Purple was now an awesome fresh force. Time was running out, and Milo could wait no longer. He gunned his mount to a powerful drive. "Kelso moved up boldly approaching the stretch," pulled away from The Axe and raced to the leader. Bill Boland on Beau Purple saw him coming. Fearing the gelding would rush past, he raised his whip and let it fall. Beau Purple responded with a surge of his own. As they entered the stretch, it was Beau Purple by two, with Kelso second. The Axe was two lengths behind, with Carry Back fifth, three and a half lengths back. The whip rained down on Beau Purple. Kelso strained to catch him. At the wire, it was Beau Purple by two lengths, in his fourth course record of the year. Kelso "finished courageously,"[51] neither gaining nor losing another inch.

The feared Axe II was six lengths behind, with Wise Ship fourth, Carry Back fifth. The French horses never had a chance. Monade couldn't find racing room, and "was not hard-ridden when hopelessly beaten."[52] Val de Loir "broke poorly and lost all chance."[53] Forty-two years later, Carl Hanford would blame himself for the gelding's defeat: "I got him beat that day. My own instructions beat him."[54]

Perhaps. But it was the son of Beau Gar's crowning achievement, his hard-won seal of approval as a serious contender for Horse of the Year honors. He had beaten Kelso in course record time, and done so at the gelding's own game: a long distance race under equal weights. He would never again be taken for granted.

It had been a long day. As I lay in bed that night, two thoughts loomed: Kelso had lost, and the world hadn't ended. A day later, the immediate crisis was over.

Remarkably, with the Washington, D.C. International only two weeks away, the Cold War never reached the racetrack. To everyone's credit, the affable Soviet riders and trainers stabled at Laurel were among the most popular and well received at the track.

On the strength of his stunning triumph, Beau Purple was invited to join Kelso and Carry Back in the eleventh running of the prestigious International. On November 12, ten horses, representing eight nations, prepared to face the American trio. It was the strongest field yet assembled in the Maryland event, and Carl Hanford had reason to worry. There wasn't a speed horse in the race to sap Beau Purple in the early stages. Allowed to run unmolested, the fleet colt would steal the race. To run with Beau Purple was suicide. To wait was equally lethal. Only one horse had the speed to run with him, and that horse was in his barn. It was a gamble. In short, it was a horse race.

Most thoroughbreds possess an all-out drive of three furlongs, able to be unleashed somewhere in the course of an event. A few horses can extend their sprint an additional furlong. Very few can sustain it longer. How and when speed is applied is determined by strategy and luck. The variables are many. The duration of maximum speed is finite.

Match II of France was accorded the best chance of upsetting the American runners. Widely regarded as European champion, he had triumphed in England's prestigious King George-Queen Elizabeth Stakes at a mile and a half on the grass. Takamagahara, a descendant of Man o' War, would be the first Japanese horse to race in the United States. Accustomed to toting 130-140 pounds, he had finished first or second in all but one of his 1962 attempts.

The state-owned Soviet horses ran as one entry. The iron horse, Zabeg, returning for his third International, had finished third and fourth in previous attempts. It was widely held he would have been second in 1960, had his rider known the procedure for claiming foul. Russia's second horse, three-year-old Livan, was a mystery but for his record: seven victories in eight starts. The rest of the field had impressive resumes, but weren't given much hope. In reality, only Match II was considered equal to the American trio.

Morning papers listed Kelso as bookmakers' choice. By the time the horses appeared on the track, the bettors had spoken. Public confidence was placed in Beau Purple. For the first time in two years, Kelso wasn't favored to win. The *New York Times* dubbed it a "race within a race"[55] likely to decide Horse of the Year honors among American thoroughbreds. Promised to be "a more thrilling and dramatic horse race than any of its 10 predecessors,"[56] it surpassed expectations.

The course was "soft" as thirteen horses approached the Newmarket barrier. Allaire duPont whispered a prayer for her gelding's safety. The tape went up. Beau Purple shot to the front as expected. The surprise was Kelso. Hell bent for leather, he was running with Beau Purple! Together on the soft track, the two horses blazed the first quarter in a remarkable 24 seconds flat. Beau Purple held the lead by a head. Milo forced the pace faster. They raced by the second quarter in :23 1/5! The heat was on; there was no turning back. Far from spent, Beau Purple maintained his slim margin. Milo pressed harder, driving as though the two were the only horses in the race. They hit the third quarter in :24 1/5. It had become a "match race"—with eleven of the world's finest thoroughbreds behind them. It was a plan that could easily backfire.

Behind them, Carry Back was third, well within range of his rivals. For another eighth of a mile, the duo maintained their scalding pace. Suddenly, seven furlongs out, Beau Purple crumbled, run into the ground at his own game. Hanford's strategy had worked, but it had taken longer than expected. The gelding's lungs begged for air. In another two-eighths, the field would close—it was time to slow the pace. Behind him, John Rotz on Carry Back sensed the kill. Kelso was vulnerable—and the time to take him out was now. Moving quickly, he thrust Carry Back to Kelso's flank. For a quarter of a mile, the gelding held his ground. Approaching the final turn, he was a length on top. Still, Carry Back came on relentlessly—to his saddle, his shoulder, and finally, his throat latch.

It was a prolonged engagement, as the two horses battled eye for eye around the final turn and into the stretch. It lasted until the eighth-pole—until Carry Back, too, surrendered. Remarkably, Kelso had sustained his drive a mile and three-eighths, a full mile farther than any believed possible. Only an eighth of a mile—220 yards—remained. The exhausted gelding drifted from the rail. It was the opening Yves Saint-Martin on Match II had been waiting for. Daringly, he gunned his mount through the narrow hole, flanking Kelso with less than 200 yards remaining.

Once more, Kelso dug in, reeling as his legs turned to rubber, and his lungs screamed for air. For forty yards, he fended off the foreign challenge. On raw nerve he battled, but the great horse could sustain his pace no longer. In those last desperate strides, Match II opened a swift length and a half and swept under the wire. Carry Back was third, four and a half lengths behind Kelso. Zabeg was fourth, another five lengths back. Beau Purple was eased to eleventh. Kelso had exhausted Beau Purple, and run the entire mile and a half at full throttle. It was one of the greatest displays of strength ever witnessed on an American track.

Milo dismounted quickly, avoiding reporters in his dash for the dressing room. While the band played "La Marseillaise," Milo sat on a wooden bench, head buried in strong hands. The famously chilly rider cried for an hour. When he finally spoke, according to Joe Hirsch, it was through tears:

> Oh, how he tried! No horse ever tried like he tried today. Ever! Beau Purple grabbed us by the throat for the first mile, and it was a bitter thing, believe me. Then no sooner had we put him away when Carry Back came up, and it was another gut-puller to the three-sixteenths pole, but we beat him off. Kelso was very tired though when Match came to him, so tired I had to move him off the rail to get him to change leads. Now I asked him for a third try, and he gave it to me. I don't know where he got it from, but he came up with it. The ground was very soft and very tiring, and he was reeling, but he tried, and tried, and tried, right down to the wire. He didn't have an ounce of anything left in him when Match drew away in the last couple of jumps. Just think how much I asked of him, and how much he gave of himself! He ran his heart out![57]

Years later, Hirsch would add: "And what a heart he had. He was Kelso, possibly the greatest American racehorse of the century. This, even in defeat, was his finest hour."[58]

By dueling Carry Back and Beau Purple into submission, Kelso had all but secured Horse of the Year honors for the third straight season. All that remained was one more victory to seal the championship, and become the sport's fifth millionaire. The inaugural Governor's Gold Plate at Garden State Park provided the perfect spot. With Kelso entered, half the field withdrew, leaving only four rivals to face the champion. Despite the presence of stalwarts Polylad and Bass Clef, track officials cancelled place and show betting.

On December 1, five distance-loving thoroughbreds lined up for the mile-and-a-half contest. Kelso broke first, and for all but a brief moment between calls, led the way. Bass Clef launched a strong run on the backstretch, surging to within a length and a half of the gelding, but Milo merely waved his stick and Kelso pulled away. He cruised under the wire five lengths on top in 2:30 1/5, shattering the twenty-seven-year-old track mark by a full second. David Alexander called it "about as effortless and nonchalant a performance as has been seen on the American turf this year."[59] Milo was again glowing: "He's a great champion. We were just galloping along. When I called on him, he really moved for me."[60] It was a triumphant note on which to end the season: "Kelso Takes $54,000 Race / 2-5 Kelso Races to Track Record."[61]

That same day, the *New York Times* ran a second racing feature on the front page of the sports section: "Game Little Carry Back Bids Good-By to Racing—Ten thousand racing fans said a fond good-by today to Carry Back, one of the most popular horses ever to grace the American turf."[62] He was the "People's Horse," a $300 son of Saggy, out of the mare Joppy. Overcoming the odds of heredity, the gutsy colt had become a national star. At two, he ran twenty-one times, setting a five-furlong record at Gulfstream Park, and capping the season with the Cowdin, Remsen, and Garden State Stakes. At three, he came on like gangbusters, capturing the Everglades, Flamingo, Florida Derby, Kentucky Derby, Preakness, Jerome, and divisional championship. At four, he lost his quest for Horse of the Year by four and a half fateful lengths at Laurel. Thirteen years later, he was elected to the Thoroughbred Hall of Fame, and at the close of the millennium, selected by a *Blood Horse* panel as one of the "Top 100 Racehorses of the Twentieth Century." Forty-five years later, his track record for a mile and a quarter at Monmouth Park still stands.

In the end, Kelso prevailed. Other challengers would follow, but by decisively besting Carry Back, Beau Purple, and Jaipur, at even weights that year alone, no one would ever question: "But who did he beat?"

For Kelso, public adoration could wait. Once again, members of his own profession named him Horse of the Year, the first thoroughbred in history to achieve that distinction three times. In his year-end summary, Charles Hatton concluded: "Like Richard the Third's steed, Kelso 'trots the air; the earth sings when he touches it.'"[63]

Kelso winning the 1963 Aqueduct Stakes by five and a half lengths on his way to an unprecedented fourth straight Horse of the Year title. (Bob Coglianese)

Chapter Six

Move Over Man o' War

B Y THE FALL OF 1962, KELSO had reached maturity. Standing just a shade over 16 hands, his slender girth had deepened to 73 inches, his propulsive hips expanded to two feet. "Regarded in the round," Charles Hatton observed, "Kelso is the slim, racy greyhound type of thoroughbred."[1] Whether by coincidence or return to ancestral genes, he appeared the archetype, a throwback to equine "greyhounds of the north"—angular strains of blooded Turks from the steppes of Central Asia. The similarities were striking: slender muzzle, pinned ears, lean neck, narrow chest, thin barrel, long loin, broad hips. Uniquely trimmed to dare the wind and devour the earth—with explosive speed, sweeping stride,[2] endless endurance, and light-footed grace—no detail was spared, no energy wasted. Lean and atavistic, like the arid land from which he sprang, Kelso was elemental.

In whole, Charles Hatton summed: "The angulation of Kelso's skeletal frame and its muscular articulation are the dynamics of a little, supple thoroughbred, one who is clipper-rigged and carries no excess cargo."[3] Overall, his dimensions had changed little, but "to the perceptive eye," David Alexander recalled, "there was a subtle difference. Somehow, he looked harder and tougher. And certainly, no one was inclined to pity him."[4]

On January 1, 1963, Kelso celebrated his official sixth birthday, and later that month, arrived in Florida for his first winter campaign. Despite his strapping appearance, many believed he was a horse running on borrowed time. Doubts persisted that a six-year-old—any six-year-old—could keep pace with younger rivals.

In 1963, few tracks equaled the grace of old Hialeah with her colony of pink flamingos rising from an infield lake. On January 30, Kelso appeared for his season debut. The event was the seven-furlong Palm Beach Handicap, and on hand to usurp his crown were Jaipur and Ridan, the two best three-year-olds of 1962. In August, Jaipur had nosed out Ridan in the Travers Stakes to capture divisional honors. This season, Ridan was the buzz, electrifying clockers with scorching morning runs.

Ridan ran to his workouts, sizzling under the wire three and a half lengths ahead of Jaipur. Kelso was fourth, two lengths behind, and the suspicion of pundits seemed confirmed: Ridan was better than ever, and Kelso past his prime.

Ten days later, the three squared off again, this time at a mile and an eighth in the Seminole Handicap. For the first and only time in his career, even the handicapper questioned Kelso's supremacy. Ridan was assigned 129 pounds, one more than Kelso, and installed the bettors' choice. In response, Kelso turned up the heat.

When the gate opened, Jaipur and Hitting Away exploded, dueling at a torrid pace for the first three-quarters. Approaching the far turn, Ridan surged rapidly to the tiring leaders. Behind them, Milo relaxed his grip. With five-sixteenths remaining, Kelso devoured the lot, sweeping to the front at the head of the stretch. From there, it was a breeze to the wire, as the gray and yellow silks of Bohemia sailed across the finish, two and a half lengths on top. The King was back—and so was the weight. It would never again come off.

On February 23, Kelso appeared for the twenty-sixth running of the mile-and-a-quarter Widener Handicap, premier event of Hialeah's handicap season. Ridan stayed home, nursing an injury, but Kelso's nemesis had returned. It was Beau Purple, and he had come to avenge his loss at Laurel. The weight was on Kelso—131 pounds to Beau Purple's 125. Still, Carl Hanford was confident, and his instructions to Milo were simple: Go out with Beau Purple, and bury him early.

It appeared he would. Beau Purple stumbled at the start, but recovered quickly and, in an instant, seized the lead. But there was Kelso, in swift pursuit—at his flank and "crying to run"[5]—as the two bore down on the clubhouse turn. What happened next defied understanding. Milo checked his mount, hauling him off the leader, and pulling him further and further back into the field. By the time they reached the backstretch, Kelso was fifth, six lengths off the pace. It had been the slowest half-mile in Widener history. When Beau Purple passed the six-furlong mark in a sluggish 1:12 2/5, Carl Hanford stared in disbelief. This wasn't the plan.

With a half-mile remaining, Milo turned him loose, sprinting past the pack in front, and surging within three lengths of the leader. "Rounding the bend, it was clear that Kelso's task would be formidable. Straightening away in the stretch, it became plain that the task was impossible."[6] Kelso strained mightily, but couldn't gain, closing only three-quarters of a length in the final furlong. Beau Purple flashed under the wire two and a quarter lengths in front.

To his credit, Milo assumed blame for the gelding's loss, but there was no discrediting Beau Purple's feat. Trainer Allen Jerkens was so moved he returned to the barn rather than appear in the winner's circle: "I just got all broken up. I keep remembering when I was a kid, working with broken-down horses. I'll never get used to winning races like this one."[7] In later years, Jerkens would be dubbed "the Giant Killer," the skilled trainer who trumped many a champion, including Secretariat twice. As for Beau Purple, owner Jack Dreyfus said it best: "We carried weight and set or equaled records almost every time. What more can you ask?"[8] Indeed. Carry Back and Kelso would later be inducted in racing's Hall of Fame. Beau Purple deserved more than a footnote in history.

Kelso and Beau Purple were scheduled to meet again in the Gulfstream Handicap, billed as the handicap race of the year. It was a stellar field—Kelso, Beau Purple, Ridan, Jaipur, Crozier, and 1962 Derby champion, Decidedly—until the defections began. At the last minute, Beau Purple suffered a minor injury and was withdrawn, as were all of the principal contenders. Ridan and Jaipur never raced again. That left only Kelso, 130 pounds, and five lightly weighted rivals to contest the mile-and-a-quarter event.

Milo was taking no chances. When the gate opened, Kelso sprang forward, and this time the pace was his. On the far turn, Sensitivo challenged, driving hard to the gelding's saddle. Milo shook his stick, and it was over. Kelso coasted through the stretch and under the wire three lengths on top. Asked if he was worried when Sensitivo came so close, "Valenzuela stared at the man: 'Are you kidding?'"[9] Russ Arnold of *The Thoroughbred Record* said simply: "The Gulfstream Handicap was little more than a good workout for Kelso."[10] Jobie Arnold wrote: "Kelso for a fourth time? Anyone who saw Mrs. Richard DuPont's three-time 'Horse of the Year' make a runaway of the $100,000-added Gulfstream Park Handicap March 16 would be mighty tempted to cast his ballot right now."[11]

Carl Hanford was more cautious: "Anything can happen. And there's no law says Kelso can keep up and in the shape he's in. They don't stay good forever, that's for sure."[12]

But some stay good longer than most. A week later, Kelso was in Maryland for the tenth running of the John B. Campbell

Handicap. And this time, the competition was stiff. Crimson Satan, brilliant when he chose, was ready to test him, as was Mongo, one of the toughest horses of the decade. The heavy weight was on Kelso—131 pounds—and this time it wasn't easy.

Gushing Wind rushed to the front, closely followed by War Council, Mongo, and Kelso, with Crimson Satan romping along in last. They continued that way down the backstretch, until Kelso made his move. Mongo went with him, and when jockey William Zakoor saw them coming, smacked War Council hard on his left side. There was no foretelling the chain reaction that ensued.

War Council ducked out from the whip, directly in front of Mongo. Mongo clipped his heels, almost going down. Crimson Satan, just starting to roll, pulled up sharply to avoid Mongo's heels. Only Kelso, clear of the trouble, continued to drive hard on the outside with dead aim on the leader. At the sixteenth pole, he passed Gushing Wind and began drawing away. It wasn't over yet. Like a demon possessed, Satan was tearing down the track, gaining rapidly—on Kelso. The finish came too soon for Satan, and just in time for the champion. In the end, Kelso prevailed by three-quarters of a length, becoming the first horse to win the Campbell carrying more than 126 pounds. For his part, Mongo never quit, finishing a gallant fourth despite his near-disaster.

It was shaping up as a contentious season, with Beau Purple, Crimson Satan, and Mongo all poised to unseat the King. But as R. J. Clark observed, the tough competition might prove to Kelso's advantage—providing a break from his heavy burdens—"since they won't have to put two jockeys and a piano on his back to bring him back to his field."[13]

K elso returned to Woodstock Farm for a well-deserved vacation, before launching his run for year-end honors. As the gelding rested, events raced forward. On the first Saturday in May,

Chateaugay upset Candy Spots and Never Bend in the Run for the Roses. Two weeks later, the order was reversed as Candy Spots brought home the Preakness. At Belmont, the garland was Chateaugay's once more, as the victorious chestnut was draped in the time-honored blanket of white carnations.

I n June, Kelso returned to Aqueduct. The three-month rest had served him well. At 1,034 pounds, Kelso weighed more than ever. The extra pounds would come off with racing, but his appearance continued to improve with age.

On June 19, Kelso took the track for the mile-and-an-eighth Nassau County Handicap, a prep for the rich classics to follow. Assigned 132 pounds, eighteen pounds more than his rivals, the headline was again his: "Kelso, 3-10, Scores Easily in Nassau County." The story continued, "Kelso sped through the stretch with long, smooth strides. Lanvin and Polylad charged at him gamely. They gained ground in the upper stretch, but not through the final furlong, although Kelso was only coasting."[14]

Despite the cakewalk, Kelso sped the distance in 1:48 4/5, three-fifths removed from the track record. It was his third straight victory, and the press applauded his performance—including his new good looks.

Two weeks later, Kelso returned for the seventy-seventh running of the Suburban Handicap, dubbed by the late John Campbell "the greatest horse race in America."[15] Named for England's City and Suburban Handicap, the event celebrated the coming of age for American racing—the 1879 triumph of Parole, first American thoroughbred to win a major British affair. By some estimates, the Suburban marked the birth of handicap racing as a major force in the American sport, and "the cornerstone upon which the 1 1/4-mile distance was established as America's championship route."[16] For all its appeal, it had proved an elusive prize.

Since 1884, only one horse, Crusader, had triumphed twice. Thirty-six years later, Kelso was attempting to make it two.

Beau Purple was scratched following a poor workout, leaving only Metropolitan winner, Cyrano, and the rapidly improving Saidam, as serious contenders. The greatest challenge was on the gelding's back—133 pounds—eighteen to twenty-three more than the field. With his "brown coat glistening in the sun like some expensive mink,"[17] he was magnificent before the gate even opened.

It was a leisurely pace, with Kelso in third, hard-held and "buck-jumping"[18] under multiple wraps. At the quarter-pole, Milo clucked in his ear. "The gelding's response was astonishing. He appeared to flip the two leaders over his shoulder as he passed."[19] Even more astonishing was his time—23 3/5 seconds for the final quarter. Despite the sizzling time, Kelso "appeared freshest of the field . . . pulling up."[20]

Charles Hatton called it "extraordinary time for the last stanza in a 10-furlong race."[21] Mike Casale wrote: "Few horses finish a long race with such blinding speed."[22] Kelso had become only the second horse in history to capture the Suburban twice. Thirty-one years would pass before we saw a third.

Hanford had considered a similar stab at the Brooklyn Handicap, but following Kelso's impressive score, there would be no avoiding Tom Trotter's justice. Kelso was shipped to Saratoga for the thirty-sixth running of the Whitney Stakes.

August 3 was Centennial Day at Saratoga, the hundredth anniversary of the fabled track, and I was there with my mother to see Kelso vie for the Whitney. We staked our place on the rail opposite the finish—as near as I could be to my hero. Skipping the sixth race, I tore behind the stands to the old elm bearing Kelso's number "2" in the coming stakes. Patiently, I waited.

A lone graceful thoroughbred loomed in the distance, striding smartly across the lawn. His sculpted head, inquisitive eye, and small yellow ribbon were unmistakable. It was Kelso, a far cry from the homely horse expected. I stood riveted as he circled under the tree; his spare body, elegant; his step, light and graceful; his dark coat, an aged mahogany that shone in the glistening light. Soon we bystanders swelled to a crowd, but the brown horse didn't notice. He stood rigid—his focus elsewhere—distant, remote, unwavering.

I don't recall Kelso approaching the post that day—whether he was calm or fractious, ambling or "on the bit"—but when the bell sounded, he was in no mood for restraint. Kilmoray shot forward, followed by Whiteborough and Sunrise County in pursuit. Behind them, Kelso was fourth, waging a private war with Milo. It continued that way to the backstretch—with Kelso "under triple-wraps,"[23] struggling to break his rider's hold. On the backstretch, Milo moved out from the rail, and there, in the middle of the track five furlongs from home, Kelso relaxed. On the far turn, the front runners contended. Three lengths behind with the quarter-pole looming, Kelso didn't move.

In a heartbeat, he pounced—devouring the leaders with one lethal burst, and emerging on top as they swung for home. Forty-four years later, the memory burns clear: the lathered neck, the resonant breath, the drumming hooves of history—as Kelso thundered past, breezing under the wire two and a half lengths in front with speed to spare. *The Thoroughbred Record* said it best: "PERFECT CASTING: An historic horse took the spotlight during the first week of Saratoga's Centennial."[24]

Days cooled, and the precision of Kelso's summer achievements grew to the raw force of autumn heroics. On Labor Day, over 71,000 fans jammed Aqueduct for the fifty-first running of the Aqueduct Stakes, and what promised to be Kelso's toughest test of the year. It was a field of worthy contenders: Crimson Satan, fresh from a smashing score in the Washington Park Handicap;

Decidedly, 1962 Derby champion; and Candy Spots, three-year-old winner of the Preakness, Arlington Classic, Florida, Santa Anita, and American Derbies. It wasn't even close. Packing 134 pounds, Kelso "busted up the race . . . in the final furlong,"[25] cruising under the wire five and a half lengths clear of Crimson Satan. It couldn't have been easier, "and as he danced into the winner's circle, not even breathing hard, a wave of handclapping greeted him."[26]

By now, Kelso had won twenty-one of twenty-four races in New York; his name emblazoned in headlines for four consecutive years. Journalists struggled to find new words to describe the gelding's deeds: "There's not much else that can be said about Kelso. . . His Actions Speak Louder Than Words."[27] He had become a local hero, and the unlikely bettors of Aqueduct had planted the first kiss of heartfelt applause. With it came a new name—not borrowed from the media or befitting his status—but a name of affection for one of their own. Kelso became "Kelly"—just Kelly—and the name stuck.

With fall came racing's weight-for-age classics. At a mile and a quarter, under even weights, few were eager to tackle the gelding in the September 28 Woodward Stakes. Still, two wild cards remained: first-class three-year-old Never Bend, fresh from a brilliant second to Mongo in the United Nations Handicap, and the formidable Carry Back, returned from a year at stud for one last attempt at the Prix de l'Arc de Triomphe. Only Crimson Satan and Garwol mustered the will to join them. The crowd poured into Aqueduct. They had come to see Kelly, "and Kelly was a sight to see."[28]

When the gates opened, Never Bend exploded—opening three lengths on Garwol in the first half-mile—running easily and running fast. Kelso was another length back, with Carry Back on his heels, and Crimson Satan on his. With only a half-mile down, all were running to beat one horse—the brown gelding with the yellow bulls-eye on his back. Milo moved early—with half the race remaining—not daring to let the breezing colt escape, and desperate to shake Satan, now breathing down his tail. Behind them, Carry Back stalked.

Kelso closed steadily on the flying leader, but with three-quarters down, Never Bend didn't slow. Behind them, Crimson Satan began to charge. On the far turn, Kelso caught the young colt, but true to his name, Never Bend didn't. "He had reeled off dizzying quarters and he still was full of fight."[29] Kelso drove to his throat latch; the stubborn colt waged on. Milo lifted his whip, and let it fall—twice—on Kelso's flank. For a hundred yards, Never Bend matched him stride for stride, but the result was inevitable. With three-sixteenths remaining, Kelso passed his valiant foe, sailing under the wire three and a half lengths in front with speed to burn.

"Once he took off," Milo said, "I just sat there and kept him going."[30] Crimson Satan made a bold charge through the stretch but couldn't catch Never Bend. Carry Back finished a disappointing fourth, another six lengths back. His trip to Paris was cancelled. Jack Price told reporters: "I can run him a few times here . . . a lot cheaper—but not run him against Kelso. No, thanks!"[31] Jockey John Rotz admitted: "I didn't think I'd beat Kelso—nobody in his right mind does. But I figured we'd be an easy second."[32]

In 2:00 4/5, Kelso had sped the second fastest Woodward in ten renditions, second only to his own record at the age of four. David Alexander reflected:

> I have no doubt at all that Kelso, despite his drab coat and well-worn footgear, is the most magnificent racehorse America has seen in 40 years. A young man who loves horses told me the other day that he envies me because I was around to see Exterminator and Man o' War race. Forty years from now young men who love

horses will be envying him because he was around to see Kelso race.[33]

In this, his fifth season, Kelso was becoming a legend. On October 19, Kelso appeared at Aqueduct for his fourth consecutive Jockey Club Gold Cup. For the first quarter-mile, Kelso ran between horses, under choking restraint with his head turned sideways. A half-mile later, even the iron-gripped Milo couldn't hold him. Past the stands for the first time, they swept to the front.

With one lap down and one to go, Kelly breezed—mane waving, tail flying, head bobbing in time to his cadenced stride. And his margin grew at will—three lengths, four lengths, five—as the quarters flew past, then six, eight, ten lengths in the upper stretch before Milo could rein him in. Eased to a canter in the final furlong, Kelso romped under the wire four lengths on top—and four-time champion of the Jockey Club Gold Cup. "He was galloping today," Milo told reporters. "He could have beaten his own track record if we'd tried." No doubt. Quite possibly, no horse ever lived that could have beaten Kelso that Indian summer afternoon. Mike Casale recorded,

> This was about as easy a race as the popular son of Your Host has ever won. His rider, Ismael Valenzuela, had a choking hold on him, throughout the two-mile weight-for-age test; Kelso was virtually eased up to a walk in the final furlong, yet had four lengths to spare on . . . Guadalcanal. . . . He sets a record each time he runs, it seems. Kelso is the first horse to win a stakes four times in a row since the idol of yesteryear, Exterminator, also a gelding, won the Saratoga Cup in consecutive years, 1919–1922.[34]

Kelso was picture-perfect on those golden afternoons—bobbing on and on as though he could run forever—skipping past the stands once, around for a victory lap, and past them again. And he made it look so easy with that long airy stride barely skimming the surface before rising again. A "unique, stylized way of going," Charles Hatton would say.[35] "Light on his feet," Carl Hanford described.[36] "The most beautiful thing alive," wrote David Alexander.[37]

Kelso was a different horse when the weight came off—make no mistake about it. For all his handicap prowess, one only needed to see the Kelso that emerged each fall under weight-for-age conditions to be reminded of the science of handicapping, and the truth of Eddie Arcaro's words: "130 pounds is the breaking point."

The Jockey Club Gold Cup marked Kelso's eighth straight victory, his twenty-third win in New York, and his thirtieth triumph in thirty-nine contests on the dirt surface of a main course. His legion of fans was growing, as was his reputation:

MOVE OVER MAN O' WAR

After four years of brilliant performances Kelso must be ranked at the top of the list of U.S. Thoroughbreds, up there with Big Red himself.

Kelso is more than just a great racehorse. As his country's four-time Horse of the Year, Kelso belongs at the very top of the list, on the same pedestal as Man o' War himself. This covers a lot of territory and a lot of champion performers, including two other great geldings of different eras, Exterminator and Armed. It puts Kelso ahead of such old-timers as Sysonby and Colin and Equipoise, ahead of Seabiscuit, War Admiral, Whirlaway, Count Fleet, Assault, and Citation, and ahead of such contemporaries as Tom Fool, Native Dancer, Swaps, Nashua and Round Table.

Kelso has earned his rank the hard way. He has outrun sprinters at their game and outdistanced distance horses in the classic game. He has done it carrying top weights . . . and in many of his handicap victories he has given away more than 20 pounds to his rivals.

Since 1960, the cream of four crops has taken a whack at this gifted son of Your Host, and now at the end of another campaign it is the same old story: Kelso on top, the rest nowhere. At weight for age, over a mile and a half or beyond on a dirt track, he probably is the best horse that ever lived.[38]

Once again, Kelso was invited to participate in the mile-and-a-half Washington, D.C. International. Kelso was also scheduled to appear on the grass in the Man o' War Stakes at Aqueduct, but with the International only nine days later, Hanford had second thoughts. Toes and stickers (raised metal surfaces on the bottom of racing plates, used to obtain better grip) were forbidden on the Aqueduct turf, but permitted at Laurel, requiring a change of footwear. "I don't like to change his shoes so often," Hanford admitted.[39] The record bore him out. Earlier that year, Kelso had become the first horse known to win back-to-back stakes in the same pair of shoes.

Only one blemish remained on Kelso's record—his performance on a grass surface. Despite stellar second-place finishes, the fact remained: on turf, Kelso was 0-3 in stakes competition. Debate raged whether Kelso was as good on grass as he was on dirt, and opinions varied—even among those closest to him.

Carl Hanford insisted his near misses, against the best horses in the world, spoke for themselves. Eddie Arcaro wasn't so sure. Following his loss to T.V. Lark, he was the picture of grace—until John Longden boasted his mount could beat him on dirt. When word reached him, Arcaro flashed: "My horse runs a hell of a lot better on the dirt. The Gallant Fox is next Saturday. T.V. Lark can get in it."[40] The next day, Kelso was sidelined with injuries, and neither horse ran.

Milo was cautious. "Yes, I think this horse will run over any track, but only as long as he get hold of it. . . . On grass I think he does a lot better when it's real firm, not wet or soft."[41] David Alexander proffered his own opinion:

> Kelso is not a grass horse. It's my own opinion that running over turf is a handicap to him that is equal to at least 10 pounds in weight. . . . If he overcomes his allergy to grass. . . and wins decisively over the best horses Europe can muster against him, a great many racegoers who already suspect he is one of the greatest horses of all time may conclude he is the best there ever was.[42]

The International on Veterans' Day attracted major media attention, with representatives from seven nations ready to tackle America's best. All eyes were on Kelso, and the *New York Times* ran a human interest story:

> KELSO BITING HAND THAT FEEDS HIM
> Gelding, Edgy as Usual Before Race, Makes Owner More So During Drill
> Kelso is a little crabby these days, a bit on edge. If a stranger leans too far into the stall, Kelso might bite his head off. Anyone who stands behind Kelso runs the risk of missing his performance in tomorrow's Washington D.C. International. . . . "Oh my goodness," said Mrs. Richard C. DuPont . . . "How could anyone help liking that horse?"
> All morning long, she sat in the front seat of a gray Corvair station wagon, sewing a sampler and glancing

up at Kelso's stall. Earlier, when Kelso was schooled at the Newmarket tape, she betrayed more nervousness. Eddie Blind, Laurel's starter, calmly pulled Kelso's head toward the tape. "I can't watch, I can't watch," said Mrs. duPont, hiding her face in her arms. . . . Nobody laughed when Blind pulled Kelso to the tape and said: "If he doesn't win this year, we'll fatten him up and eat him for Christmas."[43]

On Veterans' Day, November 11, ten of the world's finest thoroughbreds stepped onto the Laurel track. Livan had returned from the Soviet Union with a new name, Ivory Tower. Undefeated since his loss at Laurel, he was joined by Bryansk, two-time winner of the U.S.S.R. Purse. Buoyed by Match's score, France sent two representatives, Nyrcos and the beautiful colt Misti, third in l'Arc de Triomphe. Christmas Island, winner of the Irish St. Leger, carried the banner for the Irish Republic. Hungary sent Imperial II, a powerful chestnut with fourteen victories in his previous sixteen races. One of his two losses had been to England's entry, Espresso, in Germany's classic Grosser Preis von Baden. The Venezuelan horse, Ferumbras, was the champion of South America's prestigious Simon Bolivar Classico. Rounding out the competition was an American rival, four-year-old Mongo, a superior grass horse fresh from victory over Carry Back and Never Bend in the United Nations Handicap.

For Kelso, all were wild cards, including Mongo, whom he'd never met on a grass surface. The air was thick with tension as they approached the Newmarket barrier. Kelso was turned partially sideways. Suddenly, the tape sprang.

Christmas Island burst to the front, with Mongo, Imperial II, and Kelso rushing from the outside to join. It was Mongo by three after the first quarter, with Christmas Island, Imperial II, and

Kelso tucked behind. For the next quarter, they sizzled, as the Irish colt closed the gap, challenging Mongo as they entered the stretch for the first time. Past the stands the four were bunched, and it was the Hungarian's turn to challenge. Kelso, on the outside, went with him. Christmas Island began to fall back. Around the clubhouse turn, it was still Mongo, with Imperial II and Kelso breathing down his neck. By the end of a mile, Kelso was a head behind, with Imperial II dropping back, and Nyrcos rushing to fill the void. On the backstretch, Valenzuela sat chilly, allowing Mongo to slow the pace and reopen a clear lead with only a quarter-mile remaining. Text accounts state otherwise, but the chart shows Mongo on top by three at the quarter-pole; Nyrcos was another four lengths behind.

On the far turn, it was Kelso's time to roar, and he poured it on, closing the gap as they turned for home. It was Mongo on the inside, Kelso on the out, lapped on the leader only a half-length behind. With a furlong remaining, Kelso ran like his life depended on it, but the hickory-hewn colt didn't bend. Nor did his margin shrink. On they ran—flat to the ground, ears pinned back—two horses running their hearts out. Mongo didn't yield, and the gap never closed. He flashed under the wire a half-length in front. It was another twelve lengths back to the French colt, Nyrcos.

Mongo had scorched the soft turf of Laurel, blazing the second fastest time in the history of the race—sizzling the final quarter in 23 4/5! "When horses run like that, they've got to be great (or the clock is broken)," wrote Robert Clark.[44] It was a heartbreaking loss for Kelso—his third at Laurel—but there was no discrediting Mongo. He ran like Kelso, some said. "He ran just like Mongo," jockey Wayne Chambers asserted.[45] Carl Hanford was the first to congratulate him.

The International did nothing to dim Kelso's status. On November 22, the eve of his fourth Horse of the Year crown, the champion earned a feature article in *Life* magazine: "The Iron Ugly Duckling Rides Again."[46] After four years of waiting, celebrity was brief. . . . On that same day, just past noon, the life of President John F. Kennedy was stilled by an assassin's bullet on the streets of Dallas, Texas. A pall settled over the nation.

On November 25, Kelso was unanimously elected Horse of the Year, the only thoroughbred in history to achieve that accolade four times. For his part, Mongo was selected Best Grass Horse. Likely, few noticed. Only one horse that year was destined to live in memory: a riderless black stallion carrying the reversed boots of a fallen hero through the streets of Washington, D.C.

That same day, the body of President John F. Kennedy was laid to rest at Arlington National Cemetery. As "Taps" sounded over the grassy plain, and the endless salute of guns finally stilled, a curtain descended. Thanksgiving was a time of mourning. Still, wrote David Alexander, there were a few things that tragic year for which to give thanks: "The main thing," he penned, "is a horse named Kelso."[47]

With a half-mile remaining, seven-year old Kelso catches Gun Bow, beginning their epic duel in the 1964 Washington, D.C. International. (Laurel Race Course)

Chapter Seven

The Curtain Call

AGAINST THE BACKDROP OF a bereft nation, Kelso returned in 1964 at the age of seven. Following his performance at six, many now believed the gelding was impervious to the effects of age. In January, Charles Hatton asserted:

> Kelso's only point of reference is himself. . . . He seems to mock all efforts to improve-the-breed beyond his own superlative class.
>
> For four years now, Kelso has been keeping the books . . . with his flashing hoofs hammering out a record that will endure long as if it were chiseled in stone. By common consent, he is acknowledged as "one of the ones."[1]

Kelso was aging, however, and the signs were apparent to those who knew him. Gone was that push–button burst of acceleration—the cat-like pounce of youth—turned on and off at will, anywhere, at any time, in the course of competition. Carl Hanford explained:

> Age affects Kelso . . . to the extent that he has to put more effort in his races all the way now then he did from the time he was 3 up until the end of his 5-year old season. He could jog along any way he wanted to and put

in one burst of speed and fix his opposition. Now he has to put in effort all the way to get results. He is just as determined, but I don't think he has that burst of speed he used to have when he wanted it in the middle part of a race.... His ability is still there. He just has a different way of getting the results.[2]

It was to be expected. With aging, the fast-twitch muscle fibers of speed and power begin to decline, as do chemicals needed for quick energy release and short bursts of rapid activity. Soft tissue hardens, joints stiffen, and flexibility lessens. Only aerobic ability, and the slow-twitch muscle fiber of endurance, are able to retain youthful levels.

At seven, Kelso would be forced to tap vast reserves of stamina and strength, often driving from start to finish, exhausting Milo as much as himself. In his finest moments, these stores proved endless.

In December, rumor circulated that a match race between Kelso and Mongo was in the making. No sooner had the buzz begun than it ended. On January 3, Kelso wrenched an ankle in a morning workout, knocking him out of the Seminole, Widener, and all hopes for a winter campaign.

For two weeks, the gelding walked daily; for another three, he jogged in the saddling area. By mid-February, he'd had enough. "He raised so much sand yesterday that we had to gallop him this morning," Carl Hanford told reporters. "I'm doing as little as possible with him, and if he hadn't been feeling so good we wouldn't have galloped him at all..... You have to train them to what they can stand in the head, more than to what they can stand physically."[3] Kelso, it was announced, would wait for New York's Nassau County Handicap on June 17 for his season debut.

While he waited, new stars and contenders emerged on all flanks. At Santa Anita, an explosive four-year-old named Gun Bow romped off with victories in the San Fernando, San Antonio, and prestigious Charles H. Strub Stakes—by five and a half, four, and twelve lengths, respectively. In February, Mongo captured Florida's Widener, asserting his own credentials on a dirt surface. On both coasts, talented three-year-olds raised a splash of their own. A Canadian colt, Northern Dancer, captured Hialeah's Flamingo Stakes, while 3,000 miles west, the Santa Anita Derby fell to the pounding hooves of Hill Rise.

Come March, Gun Bow returned east, running off with Florida's Gulfstream Park Handicap. In Maryland, it was a show-down, with Mongo nosing out Gun Bow in the John B. Campbell Memorial, once again confirming his prowess on a dirt track. On April 25, the two met again. This time, Saidam bested both in the mile-and-an-eighth Grey Lag at Aqueduct. Mongo was second. While elders debated, Northern Dancer ran unchallenged—capturing the Florida Derby in March and the Blue Grass Stakes in April.

On the first Saturday in May, it was Northern Dancer versus Hill Rise at Churchill Downs. The Canadian colt emerged triumphant, eclipsing the track record, and becoming the first horse in history to run the Kentucky Derby in the magic time of two minutes flat. Two weeks later, he was back—this time winning the Preakness Stakes, and second jewel in racing's illustrious Crown.

That same month, Kelso rocked the racing world—jetting west on a moment's notice. His goal: the Hollywood Gold Cup in June. Likely I wasn't the only one elated. Hollywood Park was fast—scene of many American records—some set by great horses, others not. If records were made *not* to be broken, Kelso would be the right horse in the right place to do it.

On May 23, Kelso appeared for his long awaited debut—the seven-furlong Los Angeles Handicap—first major prep for the Gold Cup. Packing 130 pounds against the best handicap horses in the west, Kelso broke well, but dropped back immediately, eventually contesting only last place. The headline reflected dashed expectations: "Kelso in Stunner."

> Kelso must be human after all. The task of crossing the continent, picking up top weight of 130 pounds, and making his first start in six months, and that at a sprint distance, proved too much for America's four-time champion. . . . The 7-year-old Kelso finished eighth, beating only the weary Nevada Battler before a throng of 56,245 that turned out in tribute to the great son of Your Host.[4]

Carl Hanford seemed as stunned as journalists. Only Milo appeared undaunted—reminding reporters that the champ had been unplaced in his first start at six. "Then he got rolling and won nine races before the season was over."[5]

I, too, was unfazed. In reality, Kelso had been unplaced in his first start every year since the age of five. And he had come back big each time. His next outing would tell a different story.

On June 6, the mile and a half of the Belmont Stakes proved too much for Northern Dancer, as Quadrangle galloped home in front, two lengths ahead of little Roman Brother. That same day, hours later, Kelso reappeared—this time in the mile-and-a-sixteenth Californian Handicap. It was Sunday, June 7, my sixteenth birthday, when news of West Coast results reached New York papers. This time, even I was stunned. Kelso finished sixth, eight lengths behind the winner. Plans for the Hollywood Gold Cup were jettisoned, and Kelso flew home to his familiar quarters at Belmont Park.

In reality, Kelso didn't just run poorly in California. "For the first time in his life, Kelso simply refused to run at all."[6] Carl Hanford had seen it coming. From the moment he arrived, Kelso had been off his feed, nervous, restless, unable to relax. "He just kept looking around—all the time—his head turning this way and that," Hanford motions forty years later. "I never should have run that second race—I should have brought him home."[7] Thinking it was the strange speaker system upsetting him, Hanford rose in the middle of the night and cut the wires to Kelso's barn. It didn't help. The gelding remained on edge.[8]

On June 25, Kelso appeared for his first start of the year in New York. It was a minor event against a mediocre field, and Kelso carried the enormous burden of 136 pounds, fifteen to thirty pounds more than his rivals. He won by a length and a half, but his time was slow, and "he was puffing very hard when it was over."[9] Carl Hanford could only muster: "he ain't dead yet."[10] David Alexander expanded: "He definitely did not look like the old Kelso. . . . In a sense he was like an aging actor who knows his lines perfectly but has lost his former fire. . . . Quite a few observers were inclined to believe that Kelso is finished as a champion and that Father Time has finally taken his toll of the mighty gelding."[11]

In truth, Kelso was upstaged that day—in the sixth race—by a handsome bay colt making his third appearance in the United States. As recorded by the *New York Times*: "The Cain Hoy Stables' 4-year old Iron Peg . . . contributed a sparkling performance as he romped to victory by 13 lengths. . . . There wasn't anything to challenge him at any time, yet Iron Peg covered the distance in the remarkable time of 1:34 3/5."[12]

Ridden out an additional furlong, Iron Peg posted a final time of 1:48 2/5, only a fifth of a second off the track record. It was his third victory in three American starts, and Mike Casale of *The Thoroughbred Record* dubbed the colt "one of the fastest thoroughbreds I have ever seen under colors."[13]

That same week, four years earlier, Kelso had appeared out of nowhere to shock the racing world and emerge as Horse of the

Year for the first time. Now, it appeared, Iron Peg was on a similar path. But there was more to that day than two horses. Despite his lackluster victory and western failures, Kelly was hailed as a homecoming hero: "The volume of cheers that greeted the Old Man after his relatively unimportant score was greater than it had ever been after his most brilliant victories over truly great horses in the richest stakes."[14]

July 4, Independence Day, marked the seventy-eighth running of the Suburban Handicap. Once more, Kelso would take the track in the Suburban, seeking to become the first horse to win the historic event three times. This time the odds were against him. Iron Peg had "captured the imagination"[15] with his victories of seven, six, and thirteen lengths. And Kelso, despite his dreary record, would be forced to tote 131 pounds, 15 pounds more than his heralded young rival—the equivalent of an eleven-length head start. It was "a race that had simply everything and exploited its dramatic possibilities to the ultimate limit. . . . It had the beloved old champ who . . . seemed to be goggle-eyed against the ropes and about to go down for the slow, cruel count. It had the brash young challenger. . . a superb physical specimen, poised impatiently on the edge of glory."[16]

They were off. Iron Peg and Olden Times broke first, with Olden Times rushing to the front, and Iron Peg content to settle a length behind. Three lengths further back, Kelso was being hustled to maintain third. They continued that way into the backstretch—Olden Times sailing on top, Iron Peg breezing in second, Kelso struggling to keep pace three to four lengths behind. With five furlongs down, and five to go, Kelso began to move. It was stuttering at first—stride slowly lengthening, body beginning to flatten—but gradually, he appeared to be gaining. Rounding the far turn, Iron Peg bore down on Olden Times, and at the head of the stretch, he caught him. It was Iron Peg by a head, Olden Times lapped on top, Kelso a length and a half behind, and closing.

They came around the turn, and something was happening. It was happening almost imperceptibly, yet the crowd sensed it and reacted by suddenly becoming silent, like a throng that is witnessing a miracle.[17]

"At the eighth pole, Iron Peg, Olden Times, and Kelso . . . were set down for all they were worth. Olden Times cracked badly. Kelso swept by. . . . And now the crowd went berserk."[18] It was Iron Peg by a length and a half with 200 yards remaining, as Kelly continued his relentless charge. "The yards between Iron Peg and Kelso became feet, and the feet became inches."[19]

Pandemonium reigned. "Kelly! Kelly! Kelly!" the crowd shrieked, forgetting wagers against him.[20] Even objective observers forgot themselves. "Come on, Kelly," they screamed; "Old Man! Old Man! Old Man!" pleaded one, "Jesus, let the Old Man win."[21]

"The Old Man didn't win, not quite."[22] In the end, his valiant drive fell short by a head. But he had achieved what four years of glorious triumphs hadn't. "The usually heedless crowd, the crowd that has sometimes hissed and sometimes booed when champions have lost, was faced with the rare thing called greatness, and for once the throng fully recognized what it saw."[23]

Iron Peg entered the winner's circle, greeted by polite applause.

"When Kelso returned, it was different. . . . It was the most all-engulfing roar of approbation I have heard at a racetrack. Kelso stood there, lathered, his belly working like a bellows, and he wore a look of complete bewilderment. In all of his 32 victories, the Old Man had never heard a sound like that."[24] The puzzled horse couldn't know it, of course, but his gallant effort had rekindled a flame of hope in the soul of a drifting nation. "On the Fourth of July, he was an awesome heroic figure."[25]

Two weeks later, Kelly was back—this time for his long awaited showdown with Mongo. The event was the mile-and-a-quarter Monmouth Handicap, and all the best but Iron Peg appeared to contest the prize. Mongo had reemerged on June 27 at Delaware Park, capturing the Diamond State Handicap in a betless four-horse race. Gun Bow was fresh from a two and a half month rest. Kelso would shoulder 130 pounds; Mongo, 127; Gun Bow, 124; Olden Times, 125; and Dean Carl, 119.

When the gates opened, Gun Bow bounded to the lead, opening a quick three lengths on the field, drilling the first quarter in 22 1/5. Behind him, Dean Carl held second over Olden Times. Mongo and Kelso stalked in the rear, glued half a length apart. In front, the story was Gun Bow, sweeping past the half in 45 1/5—four lengths in front of Olden Times. Dean Carl began to drop back. Mongo and Kelso held the rear, lapped heads apart. After three-quarters of a mile, it was a four-horse race, with Gun Bow winging on top, Dean Carl bringing up the rear, and the pack in between beginning to tighten. In the backstretch, Mongo launched his drive, closing on Gun Bow and Olden Times. Kelso couldn't keep pace. Moments later, Olden Times launched his own bid, thrusting to Gun Bow's head on the far turn. Gun Bow repelled the challenge, and Olden Times, too, fell back. Now Mongo set sail for the leader, promptly leaving Olden Times three lengths behind. Kelso was fourth, another head back. Turning into the stretch, Mongo swept to Gun Bow on the outside. Behind them, Kelso was gaining momentum and closing fastest of all. Suddenly, it was a three-horse race.

Gun Bow clung jealously to the lead, Mongo bore down relentlessly, and Kelly closed at a furious clip. At the eighth pole, Mongo passed the game but spent Gun Bow. Kelso followed suit. With 100 hundred yards remaining, it was Mongo by a neck as the two rivals drove lapped for the wire. Once again, Mongo spilled his guts, as Kelly charged. And once again, Mongo plunged under the wire—the same neck in front.

Reporters wondered out loud: "Is Mongo a Bit Better Than Ever, Or Kelso a Jot Off His Greatest?"[26] For the first time, one broached the subject of retirement:

> Despite the fact that he has won only one race in five starts this year, it is absurd to believe there is any good reason to retire Kelso. Retiring him would not be an act of kindness because he loves to run and competition is the breath of life for him. Further it is likely that he will continue to show flashes of the pure diamond-like brilliance of his younger days, as he did in the Suburban, although it seems now that the handicappers must realize he is not the fabulously invincible horse he was when they assign their weights. Kelso does have an excuse, if he needs one. It is an excuse for shortcomings all of us acquire by merely living. Kelso is simply growing old.[27]

Perhaps David Alexander was right. Maybe retirement seemed like kindness only to those like myself, whose heart was beginning to break each time the old horse ran and lost.

A week later, Kelso was in New York, this time for the seventy-sixth running of the Brooklyn Handicap. Mongo bowed out, leaving Iron Peg, Gun Bow, and Olden Times to snare the spoils. Tom Trotter saw little reason to heed Alexander's warning. Again Kelso was assigned 130 pounds, eight more than Gun Bow and Olden Times, twelve more than Iron Peg. Gun Bow had been a short horse at Monmouth following his layoff; he didn't figure to be so again. In less than two minutes, the story of the season attained new heights.

The horses were in the gate—starter George Cassidy ready to send them away. Kelso was on the muscle, itching to run. Beside him, a horse rattled in his stall. Kelly mistook his movement for the start—lunging forward with 300 pounds of force against the closed steel door, crashing it open with his head, and dropping to his knees. Unable to rise, he fell back on his haunches—requiring assistant starters to help him to his feet. Once up, the gate sprang instantly, and Kelso ran dazed in a slow circle around the track. From the eyewitness account of David Alexander:

> By the time they were five furlongs out, Valenzuela was forced to do something he had never done before. He was actually lashing the old champ with his whip at a point of the race where Kelso almost always tries to take command himself and has to be restrained."[28]

Five furlongs later, they staggered home fifth, fourteen humiliating lengths behind the turf's new darling.

It was Gun Bow—blazing the most brilliant race of his career—sizzling a mile and a quarter in 1:59 3/5, a new track record and the fastest ten furlongs ever posted in New York. Victory was never in doubt, as he ran off by twelve freakish lengths, leaving Olden Times, Sunrise Flight, Iron Peg, and Kelso floundering like flotsam in his wake. Said David Alexander, "Few horses who ever lived were capable of beating the Gun Bow who ran that afternoon."[29]

Bohemia offered no excuse, leaving the press to draw its own conclusion. And the verdict, it seemed, was unanimous: Kelso, at long last, had reached the end of the line. William H. Rudy in *The Blood-Horse* asserted: "It was his poorest performance on a New York track. . . . and for the first time it appeared that his racing future might be in jeopardy. . . . He definitely was not the Kelso of old and at no stage did it appear he had a chance of winning the ancient fixture."[30] David Alexander concurred: "I became reluctantly convinced at Monmouth, when Kelso got within a neck of

Mongo and could not get an inch closer . . . that age has finally taken its toll on him and that it is quite possible the Suburban may have been his last truly great race."[31]

In August, Gun Bow continued his path of conquest, while Kelso stayed in the barn, nursing an egg-sized lump on his head—injury added to insult suffered in the Brooklyn fiasco. At Saratoga, it was Mongo versus Gun Bow again, and the battle was swift and decisive. Gun Bow roared home ten lengths in front, breaking the Whitney Stakes record for the course, and barely missing the track mark.

Reporters wondered out loud: "Is Gun Bow a super horse? Is he great?"[32]

> Gun Bow was running off the TV screen into the studio of Richard Stone Reeves, where he will serve as model for that artist's portrait of 1964's Horse of the Year. . . . His claim to the undisputed championship is based almost entirely on his scores in the Brooklyn and the Whitney. These victories, however, are among the most impressive any horse has scored in stakes in America in the past quarter of a century.[33]

For four long years, such words had been reserved for Kelso. It was the punctuation mark to Gun Bow's triumphs—and a dagger to the heart of Kelso fans. David Alexander reflected: "When Kelso returns, he'll have more than young pretenders like Gun Bow to overcome. There's been a change of jockeys. Father Time has replaced Ismael Valenzuela in Kelso's stirrup irons."[34]

In August, Gun Bow was purchased by a syndicate for a million dollars. Under new ownership, the invincible colt went west to Chicago, seizing the Washington Park Handicap, and laying waste to what little remained of the handicap division. Back east, the summer season was ending, when Kelso emerged at Saratoga for a mile-and-an-eighth contest on the grass. Under allowance conditions, the gelding snuck in with 118 pounds, his lightest impost in two years. Stalking Knightsboro until the final turn, Kelso sailed by the leader entering the stretch, and drew off to win by two and a half lengths over an ordinary field. Headlines highlighted his return, but the words beneath them hinted of glories past, not present:

> Kelso Equals U. S. Mark on Turf at Saratoga
>
> The once mighty Kelso equaled the American record for 1 1/8 miles on turf in his return to competition today.[35]

His time, 1:46 3/5, was fast—lightning fast—but so was the track, made hard by summer drought. Victory did little to dispel doubters. Even Hanford and Valenzuela appeared less than impressed: "I think he should have won by more," Hanford told reporters. "Of course, I'm pleased that he won, but maybe he needed the race."[36]

"I figured when I set him down, he'd open up eight or ten lengths on those horses," Valenzuela added. "He made his move, but not right away. He used to jump right off when I asked him to."[37] Unknown to all but his handlers, Kelso now carried a small crease in his forehead, one that would remain forever as a reminder of the Brooklyn disaster.

The stage was set for one last showdown at Aqueduct. All that remained between Gun Bow and Horse of the Year honors was the last effort of an aging, battle-scarred gelding, and a crop of three-year-olds waiting in the wings for the future Woodward Stakes.

On Labor Day, September 7, over 65,000 fans jammed Aqueduct for the fifty-second running of the Aqueduct Stakes. Understandably, the field was small. With Gun Bow entered, Iron

Peg, Olden Times, and Mongo bowed out, leaving only Kelso, Saidam, and two otherwise outmatched rivals to contest the rich event. Tom Trotter saw fit to assign Kelso and Gun Bow equal high weight of 128 pounds. Still, few believed any but Gun Bow stood a chance, and the heavy money—the smart money—was on the robust bay.

Kelso was the last horse to enter the paddock, and the two-dollar bettors of Aqueduct erupted in applause. Red Smith recorded:

> "Listen to that," said a guy in the paddock. "They know him by sight. The only time I ever heard that before . . . was when Hirsch Jacobs brought Stymie out for his last race at old Jamaica." "He had to lose to win the crowd," another man said, "proving he was only human."[38]

Gun Bow paced nervously—a rippling knot of bunched muscle poised on the edge of glory. Kelso ambled—a thin quixotic figure not lucky enough to be tackling only windmills. "Like a puppy who has learned to shake hands,"[39] he lifted his feet for inspection, placing them one by one in Carl Hanford's gentle hands. Mrs. duPont stood stoic, Carl Hanford tense. He and Milo conferred in hushed tones: "If nobody else goes after Gun Bow, go after him yourself,"[40] Hanford said. A man squeezed Mrs. duPont's arm. "Good luck," he said. "Thank you," Mrs. duPont replied, "but we'll need more than that. Gun Bow is a wonderful colt. We'll need the kind of horse that Kelso really is to beat him."[41] Five jockeys vaulted into the saddle, as five horses began their passage to the track. "Well," said John R. Gaines, manager of the Gun Bow syndicate, "this is the moment of truth."[42]

The horses were on the track now, "and as Kelso moved up past the grandstand, rattling applause followed him like hailstone on the roof. 'But they're betting against him!' a man said, incredulous. 'Look at the prices. There are 65,000 here, and 45,000 must be betting against him."[43] They were in the gate, the starter poised to send them off. Suddenly, the bell rang, the gates opened.

Gun Bow broke like a quarter horse—a bolt of charged lightning flashing to the rail. Milo tried in vain to stay with him—pushing, prodding, squeezing every ounce of speed from the champion's fiber. By the first quarter of a mile, Gun Bow had opened four lengths on Kelso, and the bay colt was only breezing. On they sailed into the clubhouse turn, Milo scrubbing, Kelso straining to respond. Ahead, Gun Bow galloped easily. At the end of the first half, Gun Bow had extended his lead to five lengths. "Nobody else was going after Gun Bow. Nobody else was capable of doing so."[44]

"Valenzuela sensed it first of course. He sensed that this animal between his knees was the kind of horse that Kelso really is."[45] They were in the backstretch now—that long, far side of the track—while Gun Bow breezed in front and Kelso charged. And Milo was getting into his mount—he was going after Gun Bow—more than six long furlongs from home. "And he felt the response, that sudden, surging, electric gathering of sinew, that lengthening of stride that he had experienced so often in the glory years and that had been so sadly lacking during 1964's summer of despair."[46]

"In the stands, Carl Hanford sensed it, too. . . The stride was Kelso's stride again, rhythmic, flowing, cadenced as a strophe."[47] He knew few mortals could sustain the drive demanded. The gamble was his—as was the onus. "'I told him to, I told him to,' he kept repeating, as if he were absolving Milo of all blame in case the strategy failed."[48] And Kelso was gaining, not length by explosive length, but inch by precious inch, and the gap between the two horses narrowed. They charged into the far turn with Gun Bow two lengths on top.

And now the crowd sensed it, too, and the great sound from 65,000 throats arose, stuttering and uncertain at

first, for the cheering throng was not yet convinced the
thing was happening. But midway on the turn the sound
was thunder from the hills, for Kelso was still gaining
and his stride was faultless and his heart was willing.[49]

By now, Walter Blum sensed it, too. He didn't need to look.
There was only one horse able to engender such a roar, only one
able to threaten his own. Blum knew exactly who was coming at
him, and he sat down to ride in earnest. Together they leaned into
the turn for home, Kelso driving to Gun Bow's flank.

The sound of jets from Kennedy airport was drowned out by
the din; the announcer's voice reduced to mute. And Kelly kept
coming. It was pandemonium at Aqueduct. The throng was on its
feet, shrieking madly, hysterically, money and bets forgotten. The
horses rounded the turn, running as one—two warriors propelled
not by legs, it seemed, but by the engulfing fury of sound.[50] Milo
raised his whip—just once—and in a heartbeat, history changed.

The stringy champion of so many fabled fields, whose
gray and yellow banner had been dragging in the dust of
late, moved by this million dollars worth of horse, and
his flag was flying high and proud again. . . . It was Kelly
by a head, a neck, a half-length as they went to the
eighth pole and at the eighth pole it was Kelly by three-
quarters of a length.[51]

But Gun Bow never cracked. When Kelso went by, Gun Bow
thrust again—not once, not twice, but repeatedly—narrowing the
gap to a slim half-length with 200 yards remaining. Kelso refused
to yield. He met each onslaught, repelled each thrust, and in those
last desperate strides, edged away. It was Kelly by three-quarters of
a length at the eighth pole, and it was Kelly by three-quarters of a
length at the wire. His time was compelling—1:48 3/5—only

two-fifths of a second removed from the track record despite the deep track of autumn. "If I hadn't been in good condition, I'd have fallen off," Milo told reporters.[52]

For a time, it seemed the cheers would never end. Grown men leapt up and down and pulled at their hair. Losing tickets flew like ticker tape, raining down on the hero's parade. For New York fans, it was "a bedlam comparable to the roars engendered by a homer by Joe DiMaggio with the bases filled, a knockout victory by Joe Louis or a needle-threading game-winning pass by Y. A. Tittle."[53] Even Allaire duPont, the classiest of women, forgot herself in the moment. She planted kisses on Kelso, on Milo, on the trophy presenter, on an unexpecting photographer. She stared at the stands in awe: "Why they love him. They love him almost as much as I do," she said with apparent surprise.[54] Walter Blum tendered no excuse: "What can I tell you? To get beat by Kelso is nothing to be embarrassed about. Gun Bow ran his eyeballs out. Kelso just ran his eyeballs out a little better."[55]

Writers outdid themselves with eloquence, returning always to one incredulous observation: the tribute received by Kelso was the greatest in the history of the American turf. In the end, William H. Rudy of *The Blood-Horse* recorded: "It is the champion's job to meet all comers, and Kelso has done nothing but that. In fiction, the story can end with the old and bloody champ still the champion, but in reality the day comes when he has met his match. Happily that day is not here yet, and when it does come, 65,066 people can say they saw Kel win the 1964 Aqueduct and hold off the inevitable."[56]

"Never in some 45 years have I heard a wilder ovation given a thoroughbred," wrote Mike Casale in *The Thoroughbred Record*. "Kelso was at his best. And when at his best, no horse can beat Kelso."[57] David Alexander reflected:

Kelso has achieved something very odd indeed. When he was virtually invincible, he was accepted, admired, respected. He was there, like the Rocky Mountains or the Atlantic Ocean, formidable, impressive, yet strangely remote. Only in this season of his failures, when age has touched him and slowed him down, has he finally moved men's hearts. . . . It is as if his defeats have finally made men conscious of how truly great his victories were.

In my own prejudiced view . . . the greatest horse of any of the years since Exterminator and Man o' War were around the running parks is a light-waisted, wiry, dark bay or brown gelding named Kelso, age seven.[58]

Gun Bow's record from January to August was superior beyond doubt. Still one inescapable truth remained: In three contests against Kelso, the score was even—one win each. On the other occasion, both horses lost to Mongo—Kelso by a neck, Gun Bow by five lengths. After four unprecedented years, Kelso stood, not as a champion who could be toppled by a better record, but a reigning king who must be bested on the field to surrender his crown. The stage was set for the mile-and-a-quarter Woodward Stakes— the final match for Horse of the Year honors.

Only three contenders dared face Kelso and Gun Bow: Quadrangle, arguably the best three-year-old in training—launching his own bid for Horse-of-the-Year honors, Colorado King, summer champion of the west, and Guadalcanal, the distance-loving son of Citation.

At 4:50 P.M., October 3, the horses were poised on the threshold; the question of best horse about to be answered. The gates sprung. Kelso exploded first and flying. Milo struggled to rein him back—to let Gun Bow seize the early pace. Under a chokehold of his own, Gun Bow obliged, breezing clear by a length as they passed the stands. They sailed into the clubhouse turn a length apart—riders imploring their mounts to save something for the end; mounts straining to break free—caution unheeded—to contest every inch from break to finish.[59] For a mile and a quarter, no more than a length and a half ever split the two. Into the backstretch and down the straightaway they soared—Gun Bow hard held and cruising, Kelso visibly pressed to stay on his heels. Behind them, Quadrangle menaced.

On the far turn, the three poured it on. Blum released his hold, Milo set sail for Gun Bow, and Quadrangle charged—only a head behind Kelso. The crowd was on its feet, as Milo hunched lower, arms pumping, head buried in Kelly's mane. And Kelly responded—momentum building—as he drew even with the muscled bay! On the rail, Quadrangle moved with him.

They were three horses abreast turning for home—Quadrangle on the inside, Kelso on the out, Gun Bow wedged between. The trio tightened as they made the turn. Quadrangle lost room on the rail, and fell back. It was Gun Bow and Kelso—the awaited clash of titans—in the run for the wire.

Head and head, eyeball to eyeball, sworn enemies at each other's throats, two horses tore down the stretch as one. Fifty yards, a hundred . . . With a furlong remaining, Kelso looked Gun Bow in the eye. He inched out. The crowd erupted! It was Kelso by a foot, a foot-and-a-half. There was no doubt about it—he was going by. They hooted, they hollered, they whistled, they cheered—"Kelly! Kelly! Kelly!"

Then "Kelso did something he had never done before."[60] Ears pinned in contempt, he bore in on Gun Bow; he crowded him. With the speed of a striking snake, he whipped his head left. In the grandstand, Carl Hanford feared he would savage his rival.[61] Milo reacted swiftly. He switched the whip from his right hand and whacked Kelly on the left. He cocked Kelly's head to the side, pulling him out and away from Gun Bow. It all happened in the blink of an eye. But a blink was enough. In that instant, Kelso relinquished the lead. With 100 yards remaining, Gun Bow held the advantage. The cheers turned to shrieks, the shrieks to pleas—begging, imploring, Kelly to come back. And Kelly did. Resolutely, inexorably, he inched up. Gun Bow came back. Then Kelly. Together, they plunged under the wire.

No one knew who had won.

"Photo—photo—photo," the board blinked. And they waited—in the stands at Aqueduct, and in living rooms across the nation. A minute passed, two minutes, three . . . Two lathered horses paced in front of the winner's circle; waves of applause erupted from the stands; Milo and Blum stared at the board.

Another minute passed. "Dead heat, dead heat," a cry rose from the throng;[62] the phrase a remnant of heat racing, when judges with only human eyes could declare a draw—a "dead" heat—one that didn't count toward the outcome of the match. And now, with electronic eyes, the judges could do no better. They examined the photo—there was no discernable margin. They studied the mirror image—still nothing definitive. They magnified both. And there it was in the mirror—the extended flare of one horse's nostril—less than half an inch—tripping the lens.

The board ceased blinking. In that instant, Gun Bow's number went up! A roar rose from the throng. The two-dollar bettors of Aqueduct were sportsmen that day, saluting two great horses, and the epic duel they staged.

Gun Bow entered the winner's circle; Kelso returned to the barn—surprisingly cocky. "He thought he won," Mrs. duPont said later. "He went home to the barn and he thought he was victorious."[63] No doubt. When Kelso measured Gun Bow at the eighth pole that day, he knew he had him. In truth, it was harder for fans, and reporters, to accept: "Gun Bow won the Woodward by the width of a hollow-ground razor blade, and the vast majority of observers deemed that it was a dead heat even after they saw the photos."[64]

"In the days before the camera finish the decision of three placing judges could have gone either way. Out of deference to two gallant horses, judges justifiably might have called it a dead heat."[65]

"The official margin was a nose, but a close inspection of the photo showed so minute a space between them that the measurement could have been a beetle's nose."[66]

Virtually all agreed on one conclusion: "The 'moral dead heat'. . . by a micrometer measurement. . . was as good a horse race as there has ever been."[67]

The Woodward had proved much, but resolved nothing. It confirmed that Kelso and Gun Bow were equally great, evenly matched thoroughbreds. It failed to determine the better horse. That chance would return—in the Jockey Club Gold Cup on October 31, or the Washington, D.C. International on Veterans' Day.

> Only once before have two such champions appeared simultaneously and never have they met or have they been so evenly matched. . . . Perhaps we might have had such a spectacle as this in 1920 if the five-year old Exterminator and three-year-old Man o' War had ever met. . . . Kelso and Gun Bow are meeting in the normal course of events, and they are making 1964 the most dramatic racing year since Charles II's cavaliers matched their Andalusions and Arabs and common cobs on Hempstead Heath.[68]

The days grew shorter. Leaves erupted in fiery hues. Both stables accepted invitations to the International. Shortly after, Mrs.

duPont issued an announcement: Kelso would retire at the end of the season. The Jockey Club Gold Cup would be his last appearance in New York, the Washington, D.C. International his final race. Her old warrior had done enough; he was going home.

With invitations officially accepted, competing stables chose separate paths to Laurel. Gun Bow would contest the Man o' War Stakes, his first attempt on a grass course, and first race beyond a mile and a quarter. Kelso would defend his crown in the two-mile Jockey Club Gold Cup. The showdown would come in his home state of Maryland, against the finest thoroughbreds in the world.

On October 31, 51,000 fans jammed Aqueduct to bid farewell to the horse they called their own. At the age of seven, Kelso faced the toughest Gold Cup field assembled since his record-breaking score as a three-year-old. That day marked his ascendancy to the top. This golden afternoon signaled the dusk.

Opposing him would be the best three-year-olds in training, Quadrangle and Roman Brother. Neither was likely to wilt from the distance, nor shrink from a duel with the champion. Three turf specialists rounded out the field.

When the gate opened, it was Cedar Key who rushed to the front, with Quadrangle, Roman Brother, and Kelso in close pursuit. Past the stands for the first time, Kelso drew even with the leaders, and Milo glanced at the board—48 4/5 for the half, an honest pace. He returned to stalking. For over a mile, Cedar Key maintained the tempo with Quadrangle on his heels. Entering the backstretch, the grass horse began to tire, and Quadrangle assumed command. "The big three-year old was in front for a split second" before Kelso sprang, passing the two "so rapidly they appeared to be walking."[69]

Down the backstretch and into the curve, Kelso cruised on top. On the far turn, hooves pounded behind him. It was Roman Brother, charging with full fury. The quarter pole loomed. Kelso was on top by two, Roman Brother devouring the space between them. Milo glanced back. He clucked in Kelly's ear and waved his wand. In a heartbeat, all hope for little Roman Brother vanished. "There was no need for cheering, no call to scream 'Come on Kelly!' in a frenzied crescendo."[70] By the quarter pole, the race was his. Ahead lay the long corridor of an empty stage, and he the only player.

Kelso was flying now, not with the rocket propulsion of space-age flight, but with the windborne grace of a glider. It was the performance of a lifetime, a farewell of such incomparable ease and proportion, it defied known bounds of time, distance, and age. Bearing witness, 51,000 voices stilled, 102,000 hands clapped in time to his rhythmic stride. "It was an awesome sound, one I have never before heard in the United States," wrote David Alexander,

> I have heard that sound in Europe, at great music halls and opera houses, but never at a racetrack. That this form of acclaim should arise suddenly and unrehearsed from the horseplayers of Aqueduct was a small and very lovely miracle. It lasted from the quarter-pole to the finish line, and when you recognized the depth of human emotion that engendered it, it was as beautiful as music.[71]

Ears pricked to the beat, Kelso romped under the wire five and a half lengths ahead of Roman Brother, eleven and a half ahead of Quadrangle. The remainder of the field was "distanced," 33-64 lengths behind the leader. The old horse couldn't know he broke his own track record that day, or posted a new world time for a dirt track that forty-three years later still stands. But he knew the applause was for him.

In that last memorable stride, Kelso achieved possibly more in one day than any horse in modern history. He broke the money-winning record of the world. He became the only horse to win five renditions of a single premier event, besting Exterminator's record of four. And in 3 minutes 19 1/5 seconds, he cracked his own track and American records set at the age of three, running two miles faster than any horse in the world on a similar surface.

"He was running real easy at the finish," said Milo.[72] "He could have beaten his record in either of the last two cup races. . . He could have gone faster this time, too."[73] As though sensing it was his last hurrah—his final blaze of autumn splendor—passion spilled over in tribute, and onto the pages of history. From David Alexander of *The Thoroughbred Record*:

> We waited 40 years for Kelso. Nothing like him had been seen since the 1920s when Exterminator and Man o' War came close together. . . . To this battle-scarred scrivener who has seen tens of thousands of thoroughbreds run over dozens of racetracks since that day in 1915 when he perched on his father's shoulders to watch the filly Regret win the Kentucky Derby, Kelso, on many counts, has been the greatest racehorse the American turf has known. The breed, I think, is gradually improving, but I doubt I'll live long enough to see his likes again. I will definitely feel that something important has gone out of my life when Kelso walks off a racetrack for the last time on an autumn afternoon at Laurel—something of irreplaceable grace and beauty and courage.[74]

Only one more test remained for the old warrior: a showdown with Gun Bow in the mile-and-a-half Washington, D.C. International. But when it came to Laurel, Kelso was jinxed. Mrs. duPont believed it; fans believed it; even journalists seemed convinced:

There will be just one more start for Kelso . . . that
may quite possibly prove an anti-climax to the most brilliant career in the history of U.S. racing. . . . He must
accept the challenge, of course, because he is a champion
and his owner, Mrs. Richard C. duPont, is a sports-
woman.

The fitness of things demands that the Gold Cup on
a golden autumn day should have been the climax of the
golden deeds of a mud-colored horse. But the dramatic
unities of the theatre prevail no more in racing than they
do in life. Immortal Exterminator ended his career by
running third in an unimportant race against unimportant horses at an unimportant track in Canada called
Dorval. Destiny's scriptwriter is a cynical fellow whose
tongue is usually in his cheek. Kelso, at least, will make
his last appearance in a great production, and if he does
go down, he will go down fighting against great thoroughbreds from many lands.[75]

Perhaps it was true. Maybe Kelso wasn't as good on grass,
despite Carl Hanford's protests to the contrary. Maybe turf was the
equivalent of ten extra pounds of lead, as David Alexander suggested, and Tom Trotter concurred.[76] If so, there was one ray of
hope. In his own debut on grass, Gun Bow had fared no better, finishing second, beaten almost a length by the superb turf specialist,
Turbo Jet II. Possibly both horses were impeded by the foreign surface.

Eight horses from four continents and seven nations would
answer the bugle's call. The European champion, Veronese II of
Italy, was considered the greatest threat to the Americans, though
his trainer insisted "Gun Bow was the best horse in the world and
would almost certainly win."[77] Veteran Russian jockey Nikolai

Nasibov believed three-year-old Anilin, fresh from a three-nation winning streak, was the best horse he'd ever ridden, and equal to the American duo. "Three horses, Kelso, Gun Bow and Anilin," he sized up the field.[78] Primordial's trainer feared Kelso, but thought his two-time Venezuelan champion could handle the rest. The remainder, too, had impressive credentials: Japan's Horse of the Year, Ryu Forel, Ireland's Biscayne II, victor of the Irish St. Leger, and the lone filly, Belle Sicambre, winner of France's Prix Diane. Either way, the International would decide the American championship—possibly in a race that neither horse won.

Gun Bow drew post position #1 on the rail. "Perfect, that's exactly the spot we want," said Harry Albert of the Gun Bow syndicate.[79] Kelso drew #5. "'I knew it,' said Mrs. duPont. 'It's always something in the International. If only we could have been inside of Gun Bow!'"[80]

On Veterans' Day, November 11, in the fading light of a fall afternoon, Kelso paraded to the post for one last time, accompanied by a blanketed cast of the world's finest horses. "As usual the most striking horse in the parade was Gun Bow. When they pulled the blanket off, his bright bay coat fairly glistened and his knotted muscles looked like a bushel basket full of snakes."[81] Only Kelso was bare-hided. On edge and easily provoked, he resisted the blanket that bore his name. Carl Hanford relented, and groom Larry Fitzpatrick carried it proudly over his arm.

The strip was dry, hard and fast from the summer drought, as the horses approached the Newmarket barrier. Kelso was on the bit, "rank unruly," and higher than he'd ever appeared before a race.[82] Milo feared he would wheel at the tape. Anxious minutes passed as the horses settled in place.

The tape sprung, and the break was clean. On the inside, Gun Bow burst to the front "like a cannonball." Kelso shot clear of the pack and stormed to the rail. Biscayne II sprinted in third, with

Belle Sicambre a half-length back. In front, Gun Bow sizzled, scorching the first quarter in 24 seconds flat. Past the stands for the first time, he was ablaze—burning the second quarter in :22 4/5— four lengths in front of Kelso, five and a half ahead of Belle Sicambre, "running her heart out" a head in front of Ryu Forel.[83] Incredibly, Gun Bow was under restraint—Blum high in the saddle—saving his mount for the run to the wire. And his pace was torrid—amazing for any distance—unbelievable for a mile-and-a-half race. Toward the setting sun, they carved into the clubhouse turn. Gradually Milo released his hold. Slowly, Kelso inched up. The foreign horses began to drop back. Gun Bow clocked the third quarter in :24 3/5! "This was a match race now, maybe the greatest since Eclipse beat Henry in four-mile heats."[84]

They entered the backstretch, Gun Bow breezing on top, Kelso under pressure to stay within range. Suddenly, Milo's "elbows began to pump, the reins went looser and Kelso set sail for the greatest rival he'd ever known"—three-quarters of a mile from home.[85] He wasn't going down without a fight.

And so he ran—ears pinned in defiance—while the crowd roared. And slowly, the years fell away. . . . On a surface as dry and sparse as the steppes of his forebears, he was running with wild resolve. And he was gaining—no longer inch by inch as he had in the Aqueduct and Woodward—but with the rush of old, the freshness of youth, as though he might make the miracle happen one last time. With more than a half-mile remaining, Kelso loomed on Gun Bow's flank—and still he charged. The milepost flashed past, two heads bobbing in unison. The head in front was Kelso's, and the time was his—1:34 2/5—track record for the distance with a half-mile remaining!

"From that point on, down the backstretch and around the turn, it was a battle of champions, a sustained moment of breathtaking suspense, as first one head and then the other nodded down in front."[86] They broke the beam for a mile and a quarter[87] in two minutes flat—a record pace—and now the neck in front was Kelso's, and the field was falling behind. Only a quarter-mile remained—the "quarter that kills"—and already Kelso had been sprinting a full half-mile. . . .

They rounded the tight turn into the stretch—Kelso on the outside, Gun Bow on the rail—horses and riders straining for all they were worth. Despite the fatal pace, no foreigner appeared, and for a moment it appeared another epic duel. Then remarkably, Kelso edged out. At the top of the stretch, Gun Bow drifted from the rail, brushing Kelso slightly. "You don't rough old Kelso up without him coming back at you and he tried to go in on Gun Bow, and Milo's whip went down on the left, twice and hard, to keep him straight."[88] But Gun Bow never flagged and his stride never faltered. Miraculously, Kelso accelerated.

Down the straightaway he blazed—a wild horse on fire— "making his greatest run of all, drawing off and off from Gun Bow. . . to make his complete superiority a thing beyond question, racking up time on the clock that was simply unbelievable for a horse that had already covered a mile and a quarter."[89] Three lengths, four lengths, five . . . Eased in the final yards, Kelso swept under the wire with four and a half lengths to spare.

Clockers stared at their watches in disbelief. The teletimer confirmed what they had registered—2:23 4/5—a new American record for any surface, and new world record for an oval track![90] Kelso had done nothing but gain momentum, scorching the final quarter in :23 4/5—a fifth of a second faster than the first. Cheers rained down on the champion. Starter Eddie Blind stared at the board and shook his head. "Horses," he said, "can't run that fast."[91]

Suddenly, without warning, Kelso's number began to blink, and a sign flashed on the board: "Objection." A foul claim had been lodged against Kelso for intimidating Gun Bow in the upper stretch. Allaire duPont stood stoic, a graceful woman resigned to her fate. Milo moved closer. "My number won't come down," he assured her.[92]

Films revealed that Gun Bow had drifted out; Kelso had lugged in. Neither horse was without guilt, but the incident had not affected the outcome. The objection sign went off; Kelso's number ceased blinking. After ten anxious minutes and four years of effort, Kelso was escorted into the winner's circle. Milo leaned forward and stroked his neck: "Champ, you finally made it. You are a good horse. You are the greatest."[93]

Mrs. duPont wept. Carl Hanford beamed. A blanket of laurel was draped over Kelso's shoulders. Milo waved to the crowd, and posed for photographers. The band struck up "The Star Spangled Banner." Tears flowed again. The applause seemed endless. . . . Kelso stood on top of the world.

Tribute flowed, not just from American writers, but from the European press as well. "The finest piece of horse racing I've ever seen," said Tom Nickalls of London's *Sporting Life.*[94]

Even Walter Blum had nothing but praise for the horse that beat him: "That old boy just wants to beat you. He started driving by the time we were straight in the backstretch. Can you imagine a horse standing that kind of drive? That horse is one of the greatest of all time. He has to be to withstand the drive he was under in this race."[95]

It was the swan song no one expected; a performance of such magnitude, such rare brilliance, it bordered on myth. To this day, one looks at the account and wonders, "could it really have happened this way?" And always, the answer resounds: "Yes, it really did." Recounting the event forty years later, Carl Hanford says simply, "I knew all along I had the best horse."[96]

Appropriately, on that same day, Mongo ended his own career in a blaze of glory, speeding to a new track record of two minutes flat in the mile-and-a-quarter Trenton Handicap at Garden State Park. He had defeated Kelso twice, and Gun Bow three times. His own bid for glory had ended bitterly in Gun Bow's dust at Saratoga. He was the third and forgotten champion that year.

In November, Kelso was elected Horse of the Year for the fifth consecutive season, a record not likely to be equaled or challenged. Some claimed sentiment swayed judgment. Most, however, believed the title deserved. From David Alexander of *The Thoroughbred Record*:

> Kelso left no doubt of his complete superiority. Gun Bow ran his best, and had the [International] been at a mile and a quarter instead of a mile and a half, we might have had another near-dead-heat. The added quarter showed the added measure of Kelso's superiority. At the quarter pole, Gun Bow had given all he had to give and was a beaten horse. From that point on, Kelso merely widened out. And out. And out. . . . it took Kelso's final and greatest race to prove beyond dispute that he is a better horse than Gun Bow.[97]

From *The Blood-Horse*: "After covering 10 furlongs in two minutes flat, [Kelso] burst loose with a phenomenal display of speed, stamina and class, leaving a most worthy rival in his wake as he raced the last quarter in a sensational :23 4/5. It was the fastest 1 1/2 miles ever run in America, on grass or dirt, and the finest performance of a great horse. To Kelso, justly belongs all honors."[98]

"The case for Gun Bow is compelling," Jack Mann wrote for the *Herald-Tribune*,

> Only the great ones—and precious few of them— hold their championship form across a span of 11 months. But there was Gun Bow on the grass at Laurel

in November, with California receding into history, running a race that would have beaten any horse alive.

Except Kelso. The ballot on the desk says "Best Horse of the Year" and there is only one line to fill in. It does not ask about the second-best horse of the year. Gun Bow is the champion of America, but Kelso is the champion of Gun Bow.[99]

In the span of eleven days, the five-time champion had raced three and a half miles in two races—clocking the fastest two miles in North America, moving from the main track to the grass, and speeding the swiftest mile and a half in the hemisphere. It was a feat of such fierce, unparalleled strength, it stamped Kelso forever as a horse apart.

Just two months shy of his eighth birthday, Mrs. duPont retired her aging gelding to his home on the Bohemia River. He would remain in light training, appearing publicly at racetracks only for the benefit of equine research.

Still, William H. Rudy mused: "When Spring comes to the farm, what if Kel shows a restlessness and gets that look in his eye, and during gallops strides out in the old, effortless way?"[100] Indeed. What if? In the words of Jack Mann, it had been "so much fun conquering this world, and it was beginning to seem so easy again."[101]

Malicious, despite four years and a sixteen-pound advantage, is nosed out by Kelso in the 1965 Whitney Stakes. (NYRA)

Chapter Eight

Equinox

T O THOSE ON THE OUTSIDE, journalists and fans alike, the era of Kelso had ended—fittingly as it began—in a burst of speed and daylight. For five of my sixteen years, almost half the ones I remembered, Kelso loomed larger than life—fearing nothing, daring all.

But to those on the inside, Laurel changed everything. "We don't know what we're going to do now," Carl Hanford said. "He was tremendous."[1] Mrs. duPont hedged: "I still think this is his last year, but it would be a shame to stop him when he's in such wonderful condition."[2] The pressure on her mounted—letters, phone calls, conversations with friends—urging her to postpone the gelding's retirement. "I just don't know what she'll do," Hanford confessed.

In Maryland, Kelso was a local celebrity. Weeks after his stunning triumph, a reporter from *The Maryland Horse* arrived. Allaire duPont approached the stable astride a chestnut gelding. "A brown horse ridden by a young man ambled along behind her."[3] It was Dick Jenkins on Kelso, the greatest racehorse in the world, returning from a hack in the Maryland woods. Despite their casual appearance, Mrs. duPont told the surprised reporter: "Oh no, we haven't decided to retire Kelso. It's just that he's here and I like to go riding with him. . . . Kelso's enjoying it, too. He loves it. He crosses the streams like he's been doing it all his life. And he looks around at just everything. . . . Kelso will go to Aiken this winter. He'll gallop down there with the rest of the stable. What we'll do with him next year, we don't know."[4]

The year closed, and Charles Hatton provided his annual profile of the year's best horses, beginning, as always, with the perennial Horse of the Year: "Furlongs of copy have been milled out in an effort to explain Kelso, physically and in terms of genetics. But he is a horse outside the science fiction of breeding theorem, and his form confounds those who see him as just another scrawny necked gelding. Mr. Fitz [the late great trainer, Sunny Jim Fitzsimmons] has well said it is what one cannot see that counts most in a thoroughbred."[5]

On January 1, Kelso celebrated his eighth birthday. Later that winter, he arrived at the Aiken Training Center. Had his future been determined? "We're going to let the horse tell us," Carl Hanford said.[6]

Spring arrived, and with it, the realization of William Rudy's prophecy. A hungry look had returned to Kelso's eye, and indeed, he was "striding out in the old, effortless way." What's more, he had become a handful—nervous, irritable, and itching to run.

In April, it became official. Following his fundraising tour, Kelso would return to the races, appearing first in the August 7 Whitney Stakes at Saratoga, and later in "carefully selected" summer and fall events. Frankly, Mrs. duPont said, "He's so damn cocky we just can't stand him any longer."[7]

As Kelso breezed, Gun Bow engaged in a headlong sprint to seize the empty throne. At Santa Anita, he defeated Candy Spots, George Royal and Hill Rise under high weight in the San Antonio Handicap. In April, he returned east, running off with the Donn Handicap at Gulfstream Park. From there he was on to New York, and his own quest for the Handicap Triple Crown. On Memorial

Day, Gun Bow carried 130 pounds to victory in the Metropolitan Handicap. The first jewel of the crown had fallen, rightfully, to the deserving heir.

For Kelso, there were engagements to keep—at Laurel, Keeneland, Churchill Downs, and Delaware Park—raising funds for the Grayson Foundation and the University of Pennsylvania Veterinary Center. For Carl Hanford, August couldn't come soon enough:

> Every time he went out on the track in public, he thought he was going to the post again. He'd look around for the other horses, and he'd get mad as hell when he didn't see any. He wanted something to beat. . . . When I'd send him out for a light gallop, he'd try to run as hard as he could, like he was training for a classic. You couldn't hold him back, and all of a sudden I knew he was just about reaching the peak of racing condition. You can't hold a horse there for long unless you race him, and I couldn't wait for the Whitney. He was beginning to give me mean and accusing looks every time he came back from one of those lonesome exhibition gallops, and I was pretty sure he was going to take a bite out of me if he didn't go in a race pretty soon.[8]

On June 29, to the surprise of midweek fans, Kelso appeared at Monmouth Park, not in a charitable exhibition, but a minor event against seven unheralded rivals. Eight months had elapsed since the gelding's triumph at Laurel, five years since he'd run so short a race—aptly in his three-year-old debut over the same Jersey ground. Within four months of that occasion, the unlikely colt had emerged as Horse of the Year.

With Milo sitting out a suspension, Bill Boland was on board. When the gate opened, Kelso stumbled, snapping Boland's neck, and dropping back to last in the field of eight. Gradually the old legs loosened, and Kelso moved up. By the head of the stretch, he was fifth, ranging on the outside. Down the straightaway, he closed, and at the eighth pole, found his stride. . . It was a cavalry charge from there to the wire, with Cachito winning by a nose, Communique second by a half-length, and Kelso, barreling hard on the outside, third. Win, lose, or draw, this was Kelso, and his was the headline: "Kelso 3d in Jersey Dash in First Start Since Last Fall."

"Maybe he couldn't quite believe [he was racing], maybe that's why he stumbled leaving the gate," Carl Hanford told reporters.[9] "He only ran for an eighth of a mile," added Boland, "but he'd have won anyway in another jump."[10] Both were noticeably pleased.

On Independence Day, Gun Bow emerged for the Suburban Handicap, second jewel of the Handicap Crown. Inexplicably, he ran poorly, leaving a promising colt named Pia Star to run off with the prize.

On Monday, July 5, Kelso returned to Delaware Park for another exhibition. As they circled the track, his rider was hard pressed to contain his speed. Five days later, he reappeared at Delaware— this time for the $15,000, mile-and-a-sixteenth Diamond State Handicap. Despite his many years, Kelso would shoulder 130 pounds, fourteen to twenty-one pounds more than three young rivals. Milo flew in from California for the minor event, and that alone should have signaled the stable's intent. From the eyes of David Alexander:

> Kelso had never raced at Delaware before, but he had made personal appearances there twice, trotting around the track in lonely grandeur, and the crowd recognized him at once. . . . Before he mounted near the old, old tree, Milo slapped his neck three times, as much to say, "Okay,

boy. It's me again." Kelso glanced down and nodded, and Milo vaulted to the saddle.[11]

The scene was familiar. When the bell rang, Kelso and Kilmoray burst forward, with Kelso crying to run and Milo straining to hold him. Reluctantly, Kelly relented. They continued that way around the oval, two lengths behind the leader. At the top of the stretch, "Milo let the reins slither through his fingers, and in one great bound . . . Kelso was alongside the pacesetter."[12] For a moment, it appeared he would crowd Kilmoray, but Milo was ready and Kelso moved by, romping under the wire three effortless lengths in front. Had his rider let him run, David Alexander observed, the track record might have fallen.[13] "He acted like the old Kelso," Milo told Hanford. "He's as good as he ever was."[14]

Carl Hanford told stunned reporters: "He ships to New York tomorrow, and most likely will go in the Brooklyn Handicap on July 24 at Aqueduct."[15] Entered in that race were Gun Bow, Pia Star, Roman Brother, and Quadrangle, the four best horses in the nation. This was not the "carpet slipper" campaign journalists and fans envisioned.[16] To this day, Carl Hanford insists, Kelso "was never retired."[17]

While Kelso raced, Gun Bow rested, under the scrutiny of veterinarians trying to explain his Suburban performance. Until more was known, trainer Eddie Neloy was taking no chances, and Gun Bow was scratched from the Brooklyn. With Gun Bow on the sidelines, Pia Star loomed as the toughest competitor in training. In one short month, he had taken the sport by storm, equaling Swap's world record for a mile, and capturing the most prestigious handicap in the nation.

If Kelso's entry in the Brooklyn was a shock, Tom Trotter's weights were more so. The gelding was assigned 132 pounds—eleven more than Pia Star, Roman Brother, and Quadrangle. He would be conceding the equivalent of eight lengths to rivals half his age—foes that were foals the year he donned his second Horse of the Year crown. Try as they might, historians could find no instance of an eight-year-old horse winning a major American event carrying 130 pounds or more.

Neither professionals nor bookmakers gave the gelding much chance. But this was New York, and on July 26, his fans spoke. When Kelso emerged at Aqueduct for the first time in nine months, he was greeted by a thunderous roar—a wave of sound, rising, falling, and swelling again, for thirty minutes—as though acclaim alone might hold him there forever. Thoroughbred artist Richard Stone Reeves was seeing his perennial subject for the first time that year. "When the boy holds him in now," Reeves observed, "his neck is almost bowed. He looks better than ever to me."[18] By post time, Kelso was the 6-5 favorite.

Five horses shifted in their stalls. Suddenly, Roman Brother plunged forward, galloping an eighth of a mile before returning. The waiting field grew restless. "Kelso lunged and for an awful moment it seemed he might keel over backward."[19] Then they were off.

Pia Star struck the side of the gate as he sprinted for the lead. Beside him, Quadrangle challenged. For six furlongs, the big colts dueled, with Pia Star securing a slim advantage. It was three lengths back to Roman Brother and Repeating, another three to Kelso, alone in the rear. On the far turn, Pia Star disposed of Quadrangle; Roman Brother moved briskly on the outside; and Kelso moved fastest of all. With a quarter-mile remaining, it was Pia Star by a length and a half and cruising, Quadrangle second and dropping back, Roman Brother and Kelso closing hard on the outside.

They straightened for home, with Pia Star on top by three. Behind him, locked in a duel of their own, Kelso and Roman

Brother strained to catch the leader. With a furlong remaining, Kelso stalled, and a hundred yards later, Roman Brother pulled clear. But there was no catching Pia Star. He swept under the wire two lengths in front of Roman Brother, four lengths ahead of Kelso. The third jewel of the Handicap Crown had fallen as the second—to the sport's newest star. Kelso had come up "short," but under 132 pounds, no excuse was needed. A chance for revenge would come, in the Whitney Stakes at Saratoga.

Kelso was undefeated at the old Spa, but only once, in 1963, had he raced on the main course, the dirt surface known to history as the "graveyard of champions." It was here in 1919 the word "upset" entered the American lexicon, when a horse by that name toppled Man o' War. It was here too, that Triple Crown winner Gallant Fox succumbed to 100-1 shot Jim Dandy, and years later, Secretariat fell to Onion. The Saratoga strip was demanding—deep and tiring—"a track that kills off the faint of heart and weak of limb by the time they pass the quarter pole."[20] Once again Kelso would shoulder 130 pounds, and once again he would face rivals half his age. Bookmakers and heavy bettors—those with money to lose—conceded the race to Pia Star.

On August 7, the mercury at Saratoga reached 92 degrees. By 4:00 P.M., seats began to empty—as fans migrated to an ancient elm behind the track bearing the number "3." For the first time in Saratoga history, Pinkerton guards were forced to string a barrier so horse and trainer could enter the ring. "When Kelso came down the lane through the parklands . . . a roar went up that might have deceived a passersby into the belief that two horses were battling to the wire in a driving finish. No one tried to get closer. . . . They had merely come to cheer a hero, and to stand, for one miraculous moment, in the warming presence of true greatness."[21]

Between the heat, the weight, and the lessons of history, few believed their hero stood a chance. But they didn't care. "They had only their memories of Kelso who had never been beaten at this ancient heath and their hearts were so full of love for him they had missed a good race just so they could get close to the tree and see him standing there so close they could almost touch him for these magic moments."[22]

When those same fans returned to the track, they crowded the two-dollar windows. By the time betting closed, the sum of their small, sentimental wagers had installed Kelso the favorite. Carl Hanford huddled with Milo: "Make them run from the start, or given the heat and weight, they'll have too much left for us at the finish."

Riders gathered in the infield to witness the event, a tribute to the champion they had chased so many miles over so many years. They, more than any, knew a lifetime might pass before his equal would be seen again. The bugle blew; the horses took the track. From the eyewitness account of Charles Hatton: "Kelso drew a prolonged round of applause when he appeared on parade. He and Pia Star walked along proudly, like kings Richard of England and Philip of France going to the crusades, bitter rivals but to whom the restraints of the occasion prevented its expression until the starting bell rang."[23]

The horses were in the gate, the starting bell rang, and Hanford's strategy unfolded. Milo and Kelly were hustling as though they might beat the field to the clubhouse turn. On the inside, Malicious and Crewman blew past. On the outside, Pia Star rushed to secure third. Kelso was fifth, but the plan had worked. Ahead, Malicious was flying. He clocked the first quarter in :23 2/5, a swift clip for the old "graveyard," the second in :23 4/5! They sailed into the backstretch—Malicious battling Crewman,

Pia Star stalking a length and a half behind, Kelso another three lengths back. With a half-mile remaining, Kelso was fourth, four lengths off the pace. The crowd rose on cue, ready to applaud the move they knew would come. As though in response, Milo hunched lower and chirped in Kelly's ear. Ahead, Malicious was rolling, Crewman tiring, and Pia Star running easily. Behind them, Kelso "was going nowhere."[24]

At the three-eighths pole, Milo asked his mount again. Again, there was no response. A hundred yards later, it was now or never. Milo drew his whip and let it fall. The expected surge didn't follow. On the final bend, Malicious disposed of Crewman; Pia Star struggled to reach contention; and Kelso, under pressure, trailed three lengths behind. They roared into the straightaway. The deep track claimed Pia Star, and Malicious drew clear, three lengths on top with 330 yards to go.

Suddenly, Kelso woke. And at once, he fired, passing Pia Star and bearing down on Malicious as though the race was just beginning. With 220 yards remaining and two and a half lengths to close, the oppressive heat sat as heavy as the lead on his back. It was too little too late, but the fans cheered as one to lift their favorite home.

And Kelly answered—closing relentlessly—an old horse "breathing fire,"[25] and gaining with every long, powerful stride. Malicious had the advantage of four years and sixteen pounds, and he was running the race of his life—without a trace of faint heart in him. Kelly kept coming.

The gap closed to two lengths, one and a half. The roar was deafening. Bob Ussery on Malicious looked back. The old gelding was the last horse he wanted to see. He began riding furiously, his young mount giving him every drop he had. Still the gap narrowed. When Kelly reached his shoulder, the young colt's eyes were bulging, his tongue dangling from his mouth. With fifty yards remaining, Kelly was at his throatlatch. His charge would fall short, "but he was coming despite the weight, despite the courage of his adversary, as he had done so many times against so many great ones."[26] The ancient stands rocked.[27] One stride remained. Malicious would know he'd been in a horse race.

And then it happened. Kelso gathered his great body, and with "one tremendous bound" hurdled himself across the finish line.[28]

"Photo," the board flashed, as two numbers blinked. In the press box, David Alexander leapt to his feet. "That does it," he shouted, "there's no longer any doubt about it. Kelso is the greatest God-dam horse of all time."[29] Pandemonium reigned—as great as any in the history of the Spa.

It took no time for officials to examine the film. The board ceased blinking. And in that instant, number "3" lit on top! Fans collapsed into their seats. Applause followed Kelly to the winner's circle, and erupted again. When Milo and Kelso returned to the scale, they were met with the ultimate tribute—applause from the riders themselves. In the words of Joe Hirsch: "There were tears in everyone's eye at Saratoga that day, as this horse of horses came back to the winner's circle."[30]

Once again Kelso made history, becoming the first known eight-year old to win a major American race carrying 130 pounds. And once again, journalists who'd thought it was over nine months earlier, rose to the occasion. From Kent Hollingsworth, editor of *The Blood-Horse:*

> Kelso is not the horse he was at four or five. In his younger day, he had a kick, a burst of speed that could send him past any man's horse. Kelso at eight no longer has a sudden thrust. He has to be urged strongly to keep up during the early part and it takes all of Milo

Valenzuela's considerable riding skill to bring out the most powerful run in racing today.

To see Kelso wear down his adversaries in the stretch today is to see mature greatness. Kelso reminds of Ted Williams or Stan Musial in their final seasons, not the athletes of their younger days, but still better than rivals who were not even playing the game when the standouts first became champions. . . . No horse in modern time has been so good for so long.[31]

"That he may be named Horse of the Year for the sixth year in a row is quite likely, following his latest conquest," wrote Mike Casale of *The Thoroughbred Record*. "At least, there is no need to reach for the rocking chair. There's plenty of zip left in the old fellow."[32]

David Alexander concluded: "The old man drew it fine, but he got there by a nose despite eight years of living and 130 pounds on his back. All the great ones have tried him, and there've been a lot of great ones in the last seven years. He's conceded weight to all of them and beaten all of them. The old man's back and running. He's the best there ever was, maybe the best there ever will be."[33]

Veterinarians diagnosed Gun Bow's condition—an ailing loin muscle. Just shy of the weight-for-age events, the great horse was retired, regrettably without a Horse of the Year crown for which he so splendidly fought. Gun Bow was a champion—and a "great one"—failing only in the end of 1964 to unseat racing's five-time monarch. Together with Kelso, he'd been assigned 136 pounds on the *Daily Racing Form*'s annual Free Handicap—a record shared formerly only by Tom Fool and Native Dancer.[34] His rival's shadow was a long one, but thirty-five years later, the prince emerged to claim his own rightful place among great American thoroughbreds in the National Hall of Fame. Placing "Gun Bow at the top of the many great horses he rode," Hall of Fame rider, Walter Blum himself, appeared to present the plaque.[35]

Kelso returned to Long Island. With the fall classics looming, he now appeared poised for a sixth Horse of the Year title. On September 6, over 68,000 fans poured through the gates to witness the mile-and-an-eighth Aqueduct Stakes. Kelso was the reigning champion two years running in the event, and never, anywhere—on any surface—had he been defeated at a mile and an eighth. On Labor Day, the eight-year-old gelding was the horse to beat.

Seven contenders marched to the post on the recently deepened strip, with Kelso toting high weight of 130 pounds—fourteen more than Malicious, nine pounds more than Roman Brother. Once more, Malicious bolted to the front. Behind him, Pluck, Roman Brother, and Hill Rise stalked. Kelso was fifth, eight lengths behind the leader. To observers, he appeared to be "climbing."[36] To Milo, it felt like "the track was cupping" underfoot.[37] By the time they'd gone two-quarters, Kelso was ten lengths off the pace.

In front, Malicious rolled, reeling off smooth, even fractions. To the rear, Kelso labored. On the far turn, Pluck drove to Malicious, narrowing his lead to a length. Roman Brother and Kelso closed from behind. They rounded the final turn and roared into the stretch. Malicious pulled clear of Pluck, Roman Brother closed gamely, Kelso passed Hill Rise—he had found his stride.

So it appeared to expectant fans. But on this day, Kelso was merely passing a tired horse. Malicious swept under the wire three lengths ahead of Pluck, who true to his name, edged out Roman Brother for second. It was another six lengths back to Kelso. For the first and only time in seven years of racing, the son of Your Host failed to win a mile-and-an-eighth event.

A concerned Carl Hanford had no comment. Only later he told reporters: "He just wouldn't extend himself. I don't know why, but I do know there was nothing wrong with him."[38] Again, the specter of age was raised, and some thought the champion had finally tired of the game, but Kelso was beyond criticism. In the words of William Rudy: "There was no immediate explanation of his below-average showing in the Aqueduct, and maybe an 8-year old needs none."[39]

For Carl Hanford, Kelso's effort posed a dilemma. At eight, there might not be any miracles left. On Wednesday, September 22, Kelso returned to Aqueduct for an unplanned appearance in the mile-and-a-quarter Stymie Handicap. With six New York papers on strike, only 26,371 midweek patrons were on hand—many no doubt surprised to see Kelso's name on the card. For those lucky few, it would be a day to remember.

Kelso was assigned 128 pounds, fifteen to twenty-one pounds more than five contenders. It was a vital test. If the spark was still there, he would defend his crown in the Woodward. If not . . .

"Guardsmen Mounting," the bugle sounded for the sixty-second time in Kelso's career. Milo vaulted into the saddle, as one by one, the horses filed onto the track. When the sixth horse appeared, a roar of recognition erupted. Stepping lightly onto the surface was the familiar brown gelding with the yellow ribbon in his lock. He inhaled the crisp air like a tonic.

The button was pushed, the starting bell rang, and as they had for centuries, thoroughbreds charged headlong down an open stretch of ground. Duc de Great, Twice as Gay, and Repeating jostled for the lead. The pace was slow—25 seconds for the quarter—until Duc de Great shot off, spurting to a two-length advantage. He ran the second quarter in :23 3/5. Kelso was losing ground, falling dangerously off the pace. A clod of dirt flew up and struck him in the eye. The third quarter fell in :24 1/5. Down the backstretch and into the far turn they sped. Milo buried his face in the familiar dark mane. "Now, boy," he whispered. And Kelly answered. Blinking back the dirt, he swept past Twice as Gay and Repeating, and rushed to challenge the leader. By the quarter pole, he collared Duc de Great, and on the far curve, bounded by. It was Kelso by two when they straightened for home.

By the three-sixteenths pole, it was three. A hundred yards later, four. Kelly was breezing now, running "like a wild horse,"[40] and his margin grew at will—five lengths, six lengths, seven. Eight glorious lengths ahead of his rivals, Kelso sailed under the wire. Hours later, the sun passed over the equator. Autumn had arrived.

"After taking command a quarter-mile from the wire," reported Mike Casale of *The Thoroughbred Record*, "Kelso widened out with ease and was full of run at the end of the one-sided affair."[41] Carl Hanford was elated: "He still trains like a three-year old. His next race will be the Woodward."[42]

Kelso cooled out well; his eye was cleansed and treated, and he returned to the barn. Come morning, he was rubbing his eye against his body, his stall, anything in reach. Under veterinary care, the irritation cleared, but when he worked for the Woodward, his eye began to close. Protective blinkers were tried, and the eight-year-old accepted the new equipment without protest, speeding a half-mile in :47 flat. When he pulled up, his eye was two-thirds shut. Bohemia had no choice. On the morning of the Woodward, Kelso was withdrawn. In his absence, Roman Brother ran the race of his life—galloping to victory ten lengths ahead of the field.

For Kelso, there would be no Horse of the Year title, but that had never been Bohemia's goal. The real prize—the one they'd sought since spring—still lay a month away: a sixth consecutive triumph in the Jockey Club Gold Cup.

Kelso's eye worsened. "His whole eye was milk white," Carl Hanford recalled. "I've never seen anything like it. We thought he was going to lose his eye."[43] Under the best medical care—two veterinarians and a specialist who had treated Marilyn Monroe and the King of Siam—the infection subsided, but only after training ceased. With the Gold Cup two weeks away, Kelso returned to Woodstock Farm, his last quest for gold stopped short by a small bit of flying track.

Quite possibly, David Alexander proffered, "a speck of dirt accomplished what neither age, nor weight nor prowess of his foemen could achieve." He continued, "The facts are that Kelso . . . is out of competition and that there is at least a strong possibility that we may never see him race again. If the latter possibility is fact, it means that the greatest saga of American racing has finally ended. . . . Not many horses make a successful comeback at the age of nine, but then again, there haven't been too many Kelsos since the Godolphin, the Byerley, and the Darley established a line called thoroughbred."[44]

Roman Brother trumped his success in the Woodward, running off with the Manhattan Handicap by eight lengths, and Jockey Club Gold Cup by five. Hill Rise captured the Man o' War, and on Veterans' Day at Laurel, it was a one-two punch for French horses, Diatome and Carvin. At year's end, Roman Brother was voted Best Handicap Horse and Horse of the Year on the Triangle Publications poll. Kelso, Gun Bow, and Roman Brother shared high weight on the *Daily Racing Form* Free Handicap for older males. Despite the obvious analogy to his own small gelding, trainer Burley Parke was reluctant to see Roman Brother compared to the ageless wonder: "Kelso," he said in an interview, "is the greatest race horse that ever lived period."[45]

The champion's season had been too brief for Horse of the Year honors, though "few were willing to bet he could not have taken the title if able to have a full fall campaign."[46]

For three months, Kelso did nothing but rest and walk on the farm while his eye healed. On New Year's Day, Kelso turned nine, officially becoming "an aged horse." Remarkably, January 1 found him in Florida, preparing for a winter campaign:

> Kelso is back under tack at Hialeah, recovered from the eye injury which halted his training after his eight-length triumph in the Stymie Handicap on Sept. 22. Kelso at nine is still a horse to conjure with. . . . As long as he was in training, Kelso always was weighted well above Roman Brother. . . . These two may meet this winter in the Widener or Gulfstream Park Handicap.[47]

That same month, the *Daily Racing Form* published its annual summary. For a record sixth time, Kelso was profiled with the year's "Best Horses": "His vast public lionized him; his foes feared him. . . . when the mood was on him, he made it crystal clear that he still was much too much for his aspiring rivals. These were reduced to scavenging for crumbs from their sovereign's table."[48]

In February, Kelso was in the barn when Pia Star stormed off with the Widener Handicap. On March 2, he emerged for his first start of the year—a six-furlong prep for the $50,000 Donn, a stepping-stone to the Gulfstream Park Handicap.

"I won't be surprised if he gets beat, and I won't be surprised if he wins," Carl Hanford remarked. "The important thing is to get a race under him. . . . When Kelso was five, I couldn't pick a horse in the country to beat him going six furlongs."[49]

Kelso broke alertly, but dropped back quickly to eighth and last place. With a quarter-mile remaining, he was ten lengths behind the leader. Forced wide on the final bend, "Kelso roared up from last place in the stretch run," to finish fourth, four and a half lengths behind Davis II. Driven out past the wire, he completed seven furlongs in 1:24. "Good enough," said Carl Hanford, "about what I expected."[50]

What a Treat captured the featured Black Helen Handicap, but Kelso shared the New York headline, and he was the lead story:

> KELSO 4TH IN SPRINT
>
> MIAMI, March 2—Kelso, Mrs. Richard C. du Pont's famous champion who holds the world record for thoroughbred earnings, received the applause today, but the victory went to an invader from Argentina. . . . Davis II . . . finished far in front of fourth-place Kelso in a six-furlong sprint that marked the champion's first appearance in competition since Sept. 22.[51]

It was a solid start for the nine-year-old, and "it seemed to many, that Kelso was going to be the next Gulfstream Park Handicap winner, and racing's first multimillionaire."[52]

Five days later, he was working for the Donn Handicap behind a group of two-year-old fillies. Swinging for home, Kelso ran down the youngsters and burst through the pack, just as a filly swerved out beside him. He took a few bad steps cooling out, but X-rays revealed nothing serious. The following day, a second veterinarian examined the films, detecting a possible hairline fracture of the inside sesamoid in his right front ankle. Additional X-rays were taken, and a day later, the fracture was confirmed. David Alexander recorded: "He had split a little ball of bone not much larger than the pills that veterinarians prescribe for horses. The little ball which seems more like hardened cartilage than bone, is called the sesamoid and is found only in horse-like creatures. When it is split by a fracture so tiny it is called a 'hairline,' the triumphs of a champion become a part of history, for he does not race again."[53]

Kelso's right fore ankle was wrapped in a cast, and a bar shoe applied to his hoof. "How do you feel?" Carl Hanford was asked.

"Well, not as good as I felt last week," the trainer replied, "but you have to come to the end of the line sometime."[54] On March 9, 1966, Mrs. duPont made it official:

> HAIRLINE FRACTURE OF ANKLE SENDS KELSO INTO RETIREMENT FROM TURF
> "Old Boy" Has Had It
> MIAMI, March 9 (AP)-"I think the old boy has done enough," Carl Hanford, Kelso's trainer said today. He indicated there was little chance a horse Kelso's age could come back after a fracture. Kelso made his debut as a 9-year old one week ago at Hialeah Park and finished fourth in a six-furlong allowance race. It was a prep for his scheduled appearance this Saturday in the $50,000 Donn Handicap at Gulfstream.[55]

The final chapter in Kelso's long career had ended. "Kelso demonstrated the durability of class. No horse in our time was so good, so long," Kent Hollingsworth closed for *The Blood-Horse*. "His was mature greatness."[56] For *The Thoroughbred Record*, David Alexander wrote a parting tribute:

> Kelso was around the tracks for seven seasons and one more race in another season. But his running time on the stopwatch would total about two hours altogether. That is a brief time in which to make history and achieve undying fame. But it is all the time it takes to present the greatest of Shakespeare's dramas, to play the greatest of Beethoven's music, or present the most celebrated of Balanchine's ballets. Each represents perfection of its kind and Kelso's two hours approached perfection as closely as any two hours of any thoroughbred.
>
> Kelso might have retired when all his stars were in perfect apposition and all the dramatic unities had com-

bined to make his last fleeting moments on the stage [at Laurel] his greatest triumph of all.

The dramatists and novelists would say it was a sad mistake to send him back. It wasn't, because great men and great horses should do what they want to do.[57]

The cover of the November 7, 1964, Thoroughbred Record celebrating Kelso's five consecutive Jockey Gold Cup victories. (Thoroughbred Record)

Chapter Nine

Champion of Champions

IN THE TRADITION ACCORDED champions of a bygone era, Kelso and groom, Lawrence Fitzpatrick, were retired together. Spray, the gelding's lifelong track companion, and Charlie Potatoes, self-appointed canine guardian, returned to the farm with them. "It was a happy little homecoming," Mrs. duPont later recorded. "They all retired together."[1]

Kelso's leg healed quickly, and in June, the gelding was tacked and ridden alongside Mrs. duPont and Spray. Eventually, Allaire duPont herself mounted the gelding, and the two became a familiar sight, jogging the grounds of Woodstock Farm. Often they moved to the surrounding woods, hacking trails, crossing streams, and leaping logs that lay in their path. Come fall, Kelso was introduced to the chase, riding with the Vicmead Hunt Club, far back from the action of hounds and horses where he was "allowed to watch everything."[2]

That same year, David Alexander published *A Sound of Horses*, beginning with the birth of English champion Eclipse in 1764, and ending with his American descendant, Kelso:

> We began with Eclipse and when we come to Kelso,
> we have gone full cycle. Not only did Kelso, the greatest
> horse of modern times (in my opinion the greatest horse

of any time) descend directly from Cumberlands's foal in the male line, but his hopeless beginnings, his brilliant career, his effect on human beings, even his physical appearance are so strikingly similar to those of Eclipse that we feel we are reading an old, old story when we ponder the saga of this great modern champion.[3]

"This book is dedicated to a horse," Alexander noted at the start. "His name is Kelso, and he's the greatest champion the turf has ever known." Three hundred pages later, he concluded:

> I saw both Man o' War and Exterminator race (the latter many times), but I saw Man o' War when I was a child and Exterminator when I was an adolescent, and admittedly I was incapable of mature judgment. Still, I did not think I saw a better horse in the long, long post parade between the 1920s and the 1960s when Kelso reached his prime. I am convinced that Kelso is the greatest thoroughbred racehorse we have ever known.
>
> If I were asked to state my reasons . . . I'd simply tell you that I think he's done more things better on more occasions over a longer period of time than any other horse in history.[4]

The gelding had been retired a year, when Mrs. duPont contacted Alison Cram, former national junior dressage champion. Would she be willing to school Kelso in jumping and the light cavalry gaits of dressage? "Yes," came the reply, and in May, Kelso's lessons began. Alison Cram described her pupil: "He's very, very intelligent and amazingly quiet for having had such a long racing career. After three weeks, he was cantering into 3-feet-6 fences easily. . . . He stands quietly while I mount and the only time he isn't perfectly quiet is when some horses breeze by on the race track near our training area."[5]

In August, Kelso was inducted in the national Hall of Fame at the Museum of Racing in Saratoga Springs, New York. On August 10, he appeared on the track, stepping nimbly through the moves of dressage—walking, trotting, cantering—hind feet tracking in the prints of his front. With supple grace, he leaned his slender body in precise twenty-meter circles, then strode to the turf, where a jump course awaited.

With natural grace, Kelly soared into the air and descended—clearing six jumps with startling ease, tipping and dropping the other two. Despite the near misses, the old warrior exited to a standing ovation.

Six days a week, the lessons continued. Alison Cram described: "As a jumper, he's amazingly bold and very responsive to my directions. He'll jump anything I point him at."[6] "He's a real picture in his dressage movements," added Mrs. duPont.[7]

Soon Kelso was appearing at the Washington, D.C. Horse Show, and the National Horse Show in Madison Square Garden, exhibiting his leaps and figures for the benefit of equine science.

In 1967, *The Blood-Horse* published its *Golden Anniversary Edition—A Second Quarter-Century of American Racing and Breeding 1941 Through 1965*. For the twenty-five-year period spanning the achievements of Count Fleet, Citation, Armed, Native Dancer, Tom Fool, Swaps, and Nashua, it was Kelso that was featured as "Horse of the Era." Joe Hirsch delivered the tribute:

> Like the United States Marines, he proved himself time and time again, until there was nothing left to prove. He was Horse of the Year five successive seasons. He won at a mile, and he won at two miles. He won on the dirt, and he won on the grass. He won when the going was fast, and he won in the mud. He won races at 12 different tracks, under six different jockeys, and he won in winter, summer, spring and fall.

He met and defeated the best horses in training over many seasons, and he had his weight up when he did it. He carried 130 pounds or more 24 times, where Citation carried such imposts four times in 45 starts, and Man o' War nine times in 21 starts. He won 12 times under 130 pounds or more,[8] won under 136 pounds on two occasions. He was a champion of champions by any measurement, not once but so many times.

The words "champion of champions" echoed from memory. They were the same, unusually subjective words used by H. P. Robertson to introduce Kelso in his three-century chronicle *The History of Thoroughbred Racing in America*.[9] Hirsch continued:

> "There may have been horses which were faster—
> though he set seven track records and equaled two
> more—and there may have been one or two horses in
> this century which could have beaten him, in his prime,
> at level weights. Possibly. None, however, did so much so
> often, and none had more courage or the quality he dis-
> played so memorably."[10]

The manners Kelso learned from Alison Cram served him well. He continued to appear at racetracks, horse shows, and on occasion, Mrs. duPont's garden parties—sporting his yellow ribbon, and gobbling "with relish"[11] his favorite chocolate sundaes. Several times a week, he and his owner joined the chase at Fair Hill, galloping higher, easier ground to the rear of experienced hunters. Years later, Mrs. duPont reminisced: "I remember my daughter said, 'Mom, you can't do that. He will run away with you.' He was just a perfect gentleman. He was always that way."[12]

On other occasions, a different story was told: "Mrs. duPont. . . recalled with laughter the many thrills she got while astride Kelso in the hunting field. He was never an easy horse to ride, and the runs encountered on foxhunts stirred his competitive nature. He was a handful."[13] Likely, depending on circumstance and memory, there was truth to both.

In 1970, Pat Johnson and Walter D. Osborne wrote a delightful book for young readers, *A Horse Named Kelso*. Mrs. duPont provided the introduction: "Just how does it feel to own Kelso . . . is a question I've been asked perhaps a thousand times. . . . How can anyone actually possess the courage and generosity of another living creature?"

When arthritis slowed him in 1974, Kelso "was retired from the hunting field and used only occasionally by Mrs. duPont to hack around her spacious farm."[14] Old Spray passed away, and was replaced by a new companion, Pete—once Sea Spirit, winner of the 1961 New Jersey Futurity. From the beginning, the two were inseparable.

Seasons passed quietly as Pete and Kelly "grazed in the paddock, [and] ambled across the hillside."[15] In later years, "Kelso would hang his head over the top rail of a fence at Woodstock and watch young horses run on the farm track."[16] His expressive eyes held their spark. At twenty-four, a small white star emerged on his forehead, growing larger and brighter as the years progressed. Likely, the racing gods smiled. Their masterpiece was almost complete.

In 1983, at the age of twenty-six, Kelso was invited to lead the post parade for the sixty-fourth running of the Jockey Club Gold Cup, the event he alone owned. He would appear with Forego, 1974 champion, to benefit the Thoroughbred Retirement Fund. A third retiree, Pete, would walk at Kelly's side.

Eighteen years had elapsed since Kelso's last triumph in New York, and during that time, the unity of the nation had finally unraveled. Two assassinations, four presidents, and a costly war later, America limped toward stability, while a hundred miles from the capital, two old racehorses prepared to embrace their youth.

Pete and Kelly were examined by veterinarians and reacquainted with saddles, riders, and vans. Three weeks later, they were en route to Belmont Park.

In New York, Kelso posed with later champions, Forego and John Henry, for his seventh portrait by Richard Stone Reeves. "Of all the horses I ever painted," Reeves noted, "Kelso had to be my favorite, not in looks or disposition, but as an honest and great competitor. I don't think there will ever be another horse like him."[17]

October 15 dawned bright with promise, a clear fall day of deep blue and shimmering gold, and for the first time in many autumns, fans swelled through the Belmont gates. It was an occasion of once familiar routines. In late afternoon, Kelso was groomed till he shone, and a small yellow ribbon braided in his forelock. At 4:00 P.M., he and Pete were saddled in the paddock and mounted by young riders from Woodstock Farm. From the eyewitness account of Joe Hirsch:

> The great gelding . . . made a splendid appearance under tack . . . as he returned to the scene of countless triumphs for the benefit of the Horse Retirement Fund. Many veteran horsemen commented that it was hard to believe a 26-year old horse could look that fit. Repeatedly, as he circled the walking ring, thousands of fans who jammed the viewing area applauded. . . . Kelso, hearing the ovation, bowed his neck and looked ready to race.[18]

With each round of the ring, Kelso inched nearer to the crowd. At 4:30 P.M., eleven contestants, led by three retired geldings, wound their way to the racetrack. "It is now post-time," chimed the once-familiar voice of Fred Capossela, as Forego emerged to a sea of cheering fans—"strutting and holding his tail high. Kelso walked quietly behind, accompanied by Pete the Pony."[19]

When Kelly appeared, the park exploded with the same thunderous and sustained ovation that had greeted the champion's final races. Cheering crowds "lined the rail ten deep,"[20] as admirers craned for a glimpse of their heroes. Above, applause rained down in a deafening torrent. Little had changed.

For one perfect moment, nothing mattered more than an old brave horse parading slowly in front of the stands—"radiant"[21] and proud, head erect, neck bowed in acceptance of his fans' acclaim. Briefly, he unleashed a spry jog, and fans lauded the effort as they had his mighty runs. Up and down the familiar track, Kelso ambled, "stopped for a few moments to smell some flowers protruding from the winner's circle," and with applause ringing in his ears, "walked off the track for the final time."[22]

Kelso was "in high spirits" that night when he returned to Woodstock Farm.[23] He and Pete settled in the barn, and come morning, were turned out in the paddock. Checked once in the morning, and again in the afternoon, they had endured the excitement in good health.

At 4:00 P.M., Mrs. duPont escorted Sunday visitors to Kelly's paddock. Twenty-four hours after donning a saddle at Belmont, the old champion was in distress. Dr. McCarthy was summoned, and Kelso led to his stall. At 5:00 P.M., he was administered a sedative for suspected colic.

"The medication seemed to stabilize the situation," Dr. McCarthy explained. "Some of the discomfort seemed to pass and he lay down for a while."[24] Less than an hour later, the spasms returned. Kelso struggled to his feet. His pulse weakened; his body trembled; his iron legs shook. At 6:50 P.M., the gallant heart of the old warrior surrendered. Kelso expired, and with him the last enduring symbol of racing's long-distance legacy and American racing's heroic age.

Kelso was buried the following morning near his dam, Maid of Flight, in a quiet ceremony at Woodstock Farm. Years later, the stone of his sire, Your Host, would come to rest beside him. Mrs. duPont, "crushed by the unexpected and devastating turn of events, remained in seclusion."[25]

In the *Daily Racing Form*, Joe Hickey instructed:"To a generation which grew up viewing his serialized exploits both in person and on television, we say weep not for Kelso, for he went out like a champion."[26]

The champion's death was national news. Feature articles marked his passing in *Sports Illustrated* and the *New York Times*. His obituary appeared in *Newsweek*:

> Kelso, 26, the plain-looking, giant-hearted gelding who set a record by being Horse of the Year five straight times. Some of Kelso's 39 career victories brought tears to the steeliest horseplayer eyes. His death, from colic, occurred the day after a fittingly emotional farewell: the old champion paraded at Belmont before the Jockey Club Gold Cup—a prize he made his own through a half-decade in the 1960s.[27]

Today, a tombstone surrounded by stone pillars marks the champion's grave. For those who remember his unparalleled reign of grace and glory, and the eloquence he inspired, six boldly chiseled words evoke the tale:

Where He Gallops, The Earth Sings

Kelso being led by Allaire du Pont after winning his fifth consecutive Jockey Gold Cup. Kelso's trainer, Carl Hanford, looks on. (Mike Sirico)

Epilogue

A llaire duPont continued to reap honors long after Kelso's retirement. In 1983, she became one of the first three women inducted to the American Jockey Club, and in 1985, the first Maryland breeder honored by the Thoroughbred Owners and Breeders Association for breeding and racing homebreds. Six years later, she was 1991 Maryland breeder of the year. She became a Senior Olympian and gold medalist, a champion of animal rights, equine research, and conservation, and a nationally displayed needlepoint artist. In January 2006, she received *Maryland Life Magazine's* first "Marylander of Distinction Award" for her contributions to land preservation. "More than a champion of charitable causes," the journal hailed, "she is a champion in her own right."[1] But for all her achievements, in the world of racing she would be forever linked to the slight son of Your Host and Maid of Flight. Upon her death in 2006, more than one headline read simply: "Allaire duPont, Owner of Kelso, Dies at 92."

F or his part, Carl Hanford, too, was destined for tribute. On August 7, 2006, at the age of ninety, the only trainer of a five-time Horse of the Year was inducted into the Thoroughbred Hall of Fame at the National Museum of Racing in Saratoga Springs, New York. Carl Hanford's remarks on that occasion were as indicative of the man's continued modesty as they were of his abiding respect for Kelso: "There is an old saying on the racetrack that a good horse is dangerous in anybody's hands. How true that is! All of the top trainers of the past have received this honor but I don't think any one of them-and I may be a little prejudiced-have ever had their hands on a horse like Kelso. My accomplishments did not get me here today; Kelso's did."[2]

On the eve of an exhibit honoring Kelso at the National Museum of Racing, William Higgins wrote for *The Saratogian*:

> Hall of Fame trainer Allen Jerkens . . . said he was shocked when he saw Kelso's racing's shoes (on display at the racing museum) because they were so simple. "They hardly had any toe on them at all," Jerkens said. Kelso did not wear "high-tech" equipment that is common today to enhance his performance. He did it with raw talent.[3]

As time passed, accolades continued. From the *Racing Times* in 1991:

KELSO RULED WHEN THE GOLD CUP MADE KINGS

> For many years the Gold Cup was called Racing's Crowning Event, and until the Breeder's Cup it was indeed that. So much so, in fact, that in its first 69 runnings (1919-88), 64 champions contested it in the years they won their titles. . . . His [Kelso's] collective margin was 28 lengths, and in the five years he won Gold Cups he was also named Horse of the Year. A Crowning Event, indeed. And he kept setting records in the race as well. Kelso won his last Gold Cup in 1964 at the age of 7, running the two miles against a gusting wind on the backstretch. That record remains today, 27 years after

Kelso established it. Okay, two mile races aren't run that much anymore, but the Jockey Club Gold Cup was run at that distance 11 times after Kelso retired and eight champions took a run at it, including Roman Brother, Buckpasser, Damascus, Arts and Letters, Shuvee (twice), Autobiography, and Forego. None of them could beat Kelso's time or Kelso's memory.[4]

In 1998, Julian Wilson, BBC-TV's longtime authority for UK racing, authored *The Great Racehorses*, a compilation of the hundred best horses of the past two hundred years. Only ten North American horses appeared on the list. Kelso was one.

At the close of the century, *The Blood-Horse* released *Thoroughbred Champions, Top 100 Racehorses of the 20th Century*, chosen by a panel of seven industry professionals. The short list of the top five reads like a dream race: Man o' War, Secretariat, Citation, Kelso, Count Fleet.

Other listings appeared, and virtually all, with good humor, acknowledged the arbitrary nature and folly of their efforts. In 2000, the UK's *Observer* published its own list of the "ten best racehorses of all time." Adopting a worldview, only two American horses, Secretariat (#3) and Kelso (#8), were selected.[5]

In 2003, a new gelded champion emerged, sweeping to an upset victory in the Kentucky Derby, then seizing the Preakness by an astonishing nine and three-quarter lengths. His name was Funny Cide, and in June, he was favored to be the first gelding in history to capture the Triple Crown. With Funny Cide came memories of Kelso. The following appeared on the front page of the sports section in the *Boston Sunday Globe*:

HORSEPOWER TO SPARE
He was as runty and rowdy as a yearling, small and snappish and scarcely worth the stud fee it took to foal

him. . . . So they gelded him, and what emerged was King Kelly, the greatest thoroughbred of his era, and arguably the greatest distance and handicap horse of all time. . . . [W]hat was telling if you read the race charts, was how much Kelso still had in the tank when he crossed the finish line. "Speed to spare," the comments said. "Speed in reserve."[6]

In 2004, four-year-old Ghostzapper snared Horse of the Year honors, with late-season scores in the Woodward Stakes and Breeder's Cup Classic. Following his smashing 2005 debut in the Metropolitan Mile, author-handicapper Steve Davidowitz selected the "top 15 older horses since 1960," excluding three-year-old form. On top was Kelso, followed by Spectacular Bid, Dr. Fager, Forego and Seattle Slew. Davidowitz explained: "Aside from his consistency, Kelso won some races on determination that no other horse on this list could ever have won."[7]

Was Kelso the greatest racehorse in American history? After seven years of racing, he seems to have left no room for conjecture—no need to ask "what if." What if he had run in the three-year-old Triple Crown Classics? It doesn't matter–he was Three Year Old Champion and Horse of the Year, anyway. What if he'd continued to race at four? He did—and at five, six, and seven. And he was Horse of the Year each time. What if he'd been saddled with 130 pounds or more of lead, conceding vast amounts of weight and distance to his rivals? He was–twenty-four times–seizing thirteen victories, including three Whitney Stakes, two Suburban Handicaps, and the elusive Handicap Triple Crown. What if he'd been asked to run *two* miles, a half-mile further than the great distance classics of today, three-quarters further than the Breeder's Cup? He was—five times—breaking two track records, and the American record—twice—in the process.⁸ Could he have handled the world's finest horses at their own game—a mile and a half on the grass from a walk-up start? Yes, and smash the world record in the doing.

Joe Hirsch was the "dean"⁹ of turf journalists, one of the most respected racing observers for over half-a-century in the United States and Europe. In 1993, the following question was submitted to Hirsch, in the pages of the *Daily Racing Form*: "Who was America's outstanding racehorse of the 20th Century?" Hirsch responded:

> In any poll on that question there would be strong support for three horses: Man o' War, Citation and Secretariat. All would be excellent choices and for brilliance it would be hard to disagree. But our personal selection, based on excellence over a long period of time, remains Kelso. His record of five consecutive Horse of the Year titles grows larger in impact with each passing season. He held his form with remarkable vigor. At age 7, in 1964, he won the Jockey Club Gold Cup for the fifth consecutive time and his clocking for the two miles was the fastest of the five runnings. Then, two weeks later, he set a course record in winning the Washington D.C. International on the Laurel turf course. Once upon a time there was a horse named Kelso, but only once.¹⁰

Eddie Arcaro, the rider of Kelso's youth, may be the ultimate source on his standing in history. From 1931-61, he rode, or rode against, every great horse in the nation. In 1948, it was Citation, and in the years that followed, despite numerous classic victories and Horse of the Year mounts, Citation remained the best horse he'd ever ridden. The Master never wavered from that opinion—until July 1961, following the Suburban Handicap: "He's [Kelso] about as good as you'll ever see. It is hard to compare one great horse to another. I will say I never rode a horse that was so powerful."[11] The next month at Saratoga he continued: "I can't compare horses of different years, but I am sure of one thing and that is that I have never ridden a better horse than Kelso. Citation was a great horse but he was never asked to do the things that Kelso has done, weight carrying."[12] Arcaro's praise continued in September 1961, following the Woodward Stakes: "I'm not kidding. I think he may be as great as Citation. Citation was the best I ever saw or rode, and since his day I've either ridden or ridden against every other good horse in the country. If Kelso goes on winning like this I'll have to say he's as good as Citation—and I never thought I'd be saying that about any other horse."[13] Finally, in October 1961, after his second Jockey Club Gold Cup, Arcaro reflected further: "Kelso is one of the greatest—if not the greatest—horses I have ever ridden."[14]

Privately, Arcaro went further. Bill Nack of *Sports Illustrated* revealed a conversation with the Hall-of-Fame jockey during a 2002 broadcast of ESPN Thoroughbred Classics:

> Nack: "He said, 'Yeah, Kelso's the greatest horse I ever rode.' Silence. I said, 'Wait a minute. You always said Citation was the greatest horse you ever rode.' Arcaro, without missing a beat, said, 'Ah, Kelso would have kicked the s--t out of Citation!' Period. Unquote."[15]

In 2004, Cot Campbell, founder and president of Dogwood Stable and racing veteran of over seventy years, was asked by NBCSports to compile a list of the best five horses of all time. Campbell obliged, listing them in reverse order from #5 to #1: Seabiscuit, Man o' War, Citation, Secretariat . . . Only one horse remained, and Campbell left no doubt who was on top:

> Kelso was undoubtedly the greatest horse who ever looked through a bridle. No horse ever did what Kelso

did. Five times he was Horse of the Year, and he could do it all. He could go on the grass, he could go long, and he won the Jockey Club Gold Cup at two miles five times. He could sprint too. . . . And no horse did it as long as Kelso. He's the greatest horse I ever saw, ever heard about or ever will see.[16]

Kelso with Ismael (Milo) Valenzuela on top before the 1962 Woodward Stakes. (Mike Sirico)

A p p e n d i x

Kelso's Racing Record

It was an era of racing seasons that began in the spring, and extended into summer when good handicap horses were expected to carry more than 130 pounds, until autumn when the best of the three-year olds were expected to challenge their elders at weight-for-age going the championship route of two miles in the Jockey Club Gold Cup Stakes.[1]

The "proud old Cup," Charles Hatton once wrote, "perpetuated at all cost to crown the champion of champions."[2] In 1962, when his words were written, none could have imagined that the crowning route of two miles would ever be replaced by the mile and a quarter of the Breeder's Cup Classic. But generations pass and history fast-forwards, leaving only the eye of the storyteller, and long-buried accounts, to relate the past.

The raw record of Kelso's career is itself imposing, reading as William Higgins once wrote, "like someone made it up."[3]

KELSO

1957, dark bay or brown gelding by Your Host – Maid of Flight by Count Fleet
Lifetime record (1959-1966): 63 starts, 39 wins, 12 seconds, 2 thirds. Earnings, $1,977,896.

177

Horse of the Year, 1960, 1961, 1962, 1963, 1964

Champion Three-Year-Old, 1960

Champion Handicap Horse & Older Male, 1961, 1962, 1963, 1964

WON: Jerome Handicap, Lawrence Realization, Hawthorne Gold Cup, Jockey Club Gold Cup (five times), Metropolitan Handicap, Suburban Handicap (twice), Brooklyn Handicap, Whitney Stakes (three times), Aqueduct Stakes (twice), Woodward Stakes (three times), Washington, D.C. International, Governor's Plate Stakes, Gulfstream Park Handicap, John B. Campbell Memorial, Choice Stakes, Discovery Handicap, Stymie Handicap (twice), Seminole Handicap, Nassau County Handicap, Diamond State Handicap.

SECOND: Washington D.C. International (three times), Suburban Handicap (twice), Monmouth Handicap (twice), Man o' War Stakes, Widener Handicap, Woodward Stakes.

THIRD: Brooklyn Handicap.

Set new track record at Aqueduct, 9 furlongs in 1:48 2/5.

Equaled track record at Belmont Park, 13 furlongs in 2:40 4/5.

Set new track and American record at Aqueduct, 16 furlongs in 3:19 2/5.

Equaled track record at Belmont Park, 10 furlongs in 2:00.

Set new track record at Garden State Park, 12 furlongs in 2:30 1/5.

Set new track record at Belmont Park, 16 furlongs in 3:19 4/5.

Set new course record and equaled American record at Saratoga, 9 furlongs (turf) in 1:46 3/5.

Set new track and American record at Aqueduct, 16 furlongs in 3:19 1/5.

Set new course and American record at Laurel, 12 furlongs (turf) in 2:23 4/5.[4]

Remarkably, in the details of this record, lies an even more powerful story:

DAYLIGHT

Despite the slim victories of age celebrated in lore, Kelso was a horse of open daylight. In thirty-nine victories over eight years, his average winning margin was 3 1/2 lengths—4 1/2 carrying less than 130 pounds, 5 1/2 at weight for age—unextended.

SPEED

Kelso set or equaled time records[5] in 23% of thirty-nine victories, at five distances over five courses—from a mile-and-an-eighth to two miles—with speed to spare on all but one occasion.

Carrying less than 130 pounds, he set or equaled records one of every four times he took the track; one of every three times he won.

He clocked the fastest mile run by a three-year old in New York, and equaled the Aqueduct track mark for seven furlongs in a public workout.

At weight-for-age on a dirt surface, he won eight of nine fall classics, equaling or breaking track and American records four times.

In fifty stake races, he was passed in the stretch only once.

ENDURANCE

Of Kelso's fifty stake races, 24% were run at a distance of a mile and a half or more. He finished first or second on twelve of twelve occasions, scoring eight victories—equaling or breaking time records six times—by an average margin of 5 1/4 lengths.

On a dirt track, he was invincible—winning seven of seven long distance events—equaling or breaking five records over three tracks at three distances—a mile-and-a-half, a mile-and-five-eighths, two miles—by an average margin of 5 1/2 lengths.

He won five Jockey Club Gold Cups at two miles—the most wins of a single major event by any horse in history. His Aqueduct, Belmont, and American records for two miles were never broken.

CONSISTENCY

Kelso authored two winning streaks—eleven races over twelve months from three to four, and eight races over seven months at the age of six.

Despite twenty-four burdens of 130 pounds or more, he was first or second in fifty-one of sixty-three races (81%).

In thirty-nine victories, he won twenty-four major stake events, the most of any horse in American history.

Carrying less than 130 pounds on a dirt surface, he won eighteen of twenty-two stakes, fifteen of seventeen from the ages of three to six.

At a mile and an eighth, he captured ten of eleven efforts, losing only his last attempt at the age of eight.

In 1960, 1961, and 1963, he won 100% of his eighteen New York races. Though it was often said he "owned" Aqueduct, it was Belmont's long sweeping oval he loved. Closed for renovation most of his reign, Kelso won five of five contests on the historic dirt surface, equaling or breaking epic records in three.

In eight years, only five horses beat him more than once—T.V. Lark, Carry Back, Beau Purple, Mongo, and Gun Bow. Only one—Beau Purple—managed a third.

WEIGHT

Weight slowed him, but it didn't stop him. Statistics speak for themselves. Carrying 130 pounds or more, Kelso's win-loss record, margins of victory, and final time were significantly reduced, but his sheer brilliance and raw strength prevailed more times than not:

Kelso won thirteen of twenty-four races carrying 130 pounds or more, two contests carrying 136.

He won the Handicap Triple Crown, carrying more weight in faster time than Whisk Broom II or Tom Fool.

At eight, he became the first horse in American history to win a major event toting 130 pounds.

More impressive, however, is the amount of weight and distance conceded:

In thirteen victories carrying 130 pounds or more, Kelso conceded an average seventeen pounds to the second horse—the average theoretical margin of a ten-length head start.[6]

In eleven losses carrying 130 pounds or more, he conceded an average ten and a half pounds to the victor—an average 6 1/2 length margin.[7]

CLASSIC PERFORMANCE

From the ages of three to eight, one third of Kelso's stake races and one third of his stake victories[8] were at the classic American route of a mile and a quarter on a dirt surface.

He finished first or second in sixteen of eighteen mile and a quarter stakes, third in one more.

Carrying less than 130 pounds, he won six of seven races at the classic route, losing only by the flare of a nostril in his last Woodward Stakes.

At the classic *world* route of a mile and a half on a grass surface, he captured the Washington D.C. International—around three turns from a walk-up start—in 2:23 4/5, an American record for the distance, and world record for an oval track. He finished second in the same event three times. His average margin of loss was less than a length.

In his own era, Kelso's five Gold Cup triumphs were the crowning equivalent of five consecutive victories in today's Breeder's Cup Classic—a feat not likely—at any distance—to be repeated.

Notes

Introduction

[1] Warren Mehrtens rode Assault to his Triple Crown victory. Arcaro took over soon after, propelling Assault to his greatest triumphs—defeating Hall of Fame champions Armed and Stymie to secure the Horse of the Year title.

[2] Frank Phelps, "Racing Through the Century," *Thoroughbred Times.com.*

Chapter 1

[1] Most historians now believe the "Barb," one of nine horses gifted from the Emperor of Morocco to King Louis XV of France, and imported to England in 1730, was, in reality, an Arabian. I adhere to the term "Barb" to facilitate distinction of this line from the others.

[2] "Tail-male" lineage is paternal lineage, father to son, beginning with the root male.

[3] The 102 Arabians, Barbs, and Turks in Volume I of the 1891 fifth and final edition of the General Stud Book include imported stock and others foaled in England from purely imported stock. Recent genetic studies, most notably those of Dr. Patrick Cunningham of Trinity College, Dublin, have shed new light on the identity, number, and influence of foundation stock. Though many old assumptions are challenged, Weatherby's General Stud Book remains the bedrock on which the breed is established.

[4] National Museum of Racing and Hall of Fame, online exhibit, *The History of the Thoroughbred in America* (2004), p. 2, "From the Beginning: England," September 17, 2006 <http://www.racingmuseum.org/exhibits/racing-museum-tour.asp?varPage=9>.

[5] National Museum of Racing and Hall of Fame, online exhibit, *The History of the Thoroughbred in America* (2004), page 2.

[6] National Museum of Racing and Hall of Fame, online exhibit, *The History of the Thoroughbred in America* (2004), page 2.

[7] William H. P. Robertson, *The History of Thoroughbred Racing in America* (Englewood Cliffs, N.J.: Prentice-Hall, 1964), p. 7.

[8] Robertson, *History of Thoroughbred Racing in America,* quoting early pioneer Daniel Denton, p. 8.

[9] Robertson, *History of Thoroughbred Racing in America,* p. 9.

[10] Robertson, *History of Thoroughbred Racing in America,* p. 9.

[11] Robertson, *History of Thoroughbred Racing in America,* p. 15.

[12] National Museum of Racing and Hall of Fame, online exhibit, *The History of the Thoroughbred in America* (2004), page 3, "Across the Atlantic: The American Thoroughbred,"<http://www.racingmuseum.org/exhibits/racing-museum-tour.asp?varPage=9>. Heat racing was the common form of thoroughbred racing America until replaced by popular English dashes following the Civil War. It was necessary to win two heats or else distance all opponents to win the race, or *match.* Four-mile heats were the American standard. On some occasions, it required five heats (twenty miles), with only thirty minutes between, for one horse to capture two heats. Horses that finished too far behind the winner, according to a predetermined distance, were "distanced" and disqualified from further participation.

[13] National Museum of Racing and Hall of Fame, online exhibit, *The History of the Thoroughbred in America* (2004), page 3.

[14] Francis Barnum Culver, *Blooded Horses of Colonial Days* (Baltimore, 1922), p. 26.

[15] Culver, *Blooded Horses of Colonial Days,* p. 58. An expression used by New York horsemen to describe Maryland racehorses.

[16] "Distanced" refers to losing by a predetermined margin. According to Robertson (p. 14): "Sample distances were 170 yards for 4-mile heats, 130 yards for 3-mile heats, 90 yards for 2-mile heats, and 50 yards for mile heats." A horse that was "distanced" was disqualified from the contest, ineligible for remaining heats.

[17] Culver, *Blooded Horses of Colonial Days,* p. 58.

[18] Robertson, *History of Thoroughbred Racing in America,* p. 28.

[19] Robertson, *History of Thoroughbred Racing in America,* p. 28.

[20] Robertson, *History of Thoroughbred Racing in America,* p. 28.

[21] National Museum of Racing and Hall of Fame, online exhibit, *The History of the Thoroughbred in America* (2004), page 4, "The 19th Century," <http://www.racingmuseum.org/exhibits/racing-museum-tour.asp?varPage=9>. Despite their appearance, today's dirt tracks are not natural earth devoid of grass. Rather, they are scientifically constructed "layer cakes" of individual make-up. In New York, dirt tracks consist of a 3-inch sub-base of fine sand for drainage, a 10-inch base of silt and clay, and a 3 1/2-inch cushion of sandy loam.

[22] National Museum of Racing and Hall of Fame, online exhibit, *The History of*

the Thoroughbred in America (2004), page 4.

[23] Robertson, *History of Thoroughbred Racing in America*, p. 550.

[24] An additional strength in the crossbreeding formula, many American (and Australian) mares were introduced to thoroughbred stallions that could trace their own roots to the General Stud Book.

[25] Paige Howard, "A Woman of Substance, The Legacy of Allaire C. duPont," *Maryland Life*, January-February 2006, February 26, 2006, <http://www.mary-land-life.com/article_janFeb2006.jsp>.

[26] Steve Haskin, *Kelso*, Thoroughbred Legends No. 21 (Lexington, Ky.: Eclipse Press, 2003), p. 22.

[27] Charles Hatton, "Profiles of Best Horses - Kelso," *The American Racing Manual, 1965 Edition* (Chicago: Daily Racing Form, 1966), p. 103.

[28] Stephen Paul Harrison and Juan Luis Turrion-Gomez, "Mitochondrial DNA: An Important Female Contribution to Thoroughbred Racehorse Performance," *Mitochondrion*, April 20, 2006, pp 1-14, September 30, 2006 <http://thoroughbredgenetics.com/MITOCHONDRION%20APRIL%202006.pdf>. Mitochondrial DNA is DNA contained in the mitochondria, as opposed to the nucleus, of the cell. Unlike nuclear DNA, mitochondrial DNA is inherited exclusively from the mother.

[29] Ron Hale, "80 Years Ago—March 29, 1917," July 29, 2005, <http://wwwhorseracing.about.com/od/famoushorses/l/blmanwar.htm>

[30] Canadian and European race tracks run clockwise while those in the United States run counterclockwise. An important American exception was Belmont Park which ran clockwise until 1921.

[31] Under Walter Vosburgh's high-weight scale for two-year-olds, his competition was burdened as well. As a three-year-old, he carried 131, 135, and 138 pounds, always conceding great weight to his rivals.

[32] "World Record Is Set by Man o' War," *New York Times*, June 12, 1920, Sports p. 3.

[33] Ron Hale, quoting the 1947 volume of *American Racehorses*.

[34] Charles Hatton, "Profiles of Best Horses—Kelso," *The American Racing Manual, 1963 Edition* (Chicago: Daily Racing Form, 1963), p. 126.

[35] *Thoroughbred Champions, Top 100 Racehorses of the 20th Century*, p. 26.

[36] Marvin Drager, "Count Fleet," *The Most Glorious Crown* (New York: Charles Scribner's Sons, 1975), p. 109.

[37] Hale, quoting the 1947 volume of *American Racehorses*, p. 111.

[38] Drager, "Count Fleet," p. 111.

[39] Drager, quoting Robert Kelley, "Count Fleet," p. 111.

[40] Drager, quoting Arthur Daly, "Count Fleet," p. 111.

[41] Drager, quoting the Associated Press, "Count Fleet," p. 113.

[42] Drager, "Count Fleet," p. 115.

[43] From official chart of the 1943 Belmont Stakes. Drager, "Count Fleet," p. 119.

[44] *Thoroughbred Champion, Top 100 Racehorses of the 20th Century*, p. 29.

[45] Liz Martiniak, "Hampton," *Thoroughbred Heritage, Portraits*, September 6, 2006, <http://www.tbheritage.com/Portraits/Hampton.html>.

[46] Presumably at Scotland's historic Kelso Racecourse, a seat of British flat racing until 1888.

[47] Martiniak, "Hampton."

[48] Elizabeth Martiniak, "Bayardo," *Thoroughbred Heritage, Portraits*, September 6, 2006, <http://www.tbheritage.com/Portraits/Bayardo.html>.

[49] Martiniak, "Bayardo."

[50] Anne Peters, "Hyperion," *Thoroughbred Heritage, Portraits*, September 6, 2006, <http://www.tbheritage.com/Portraits/Hyperion.html>.

[51] A hand is unit of measure equaling four inches, used exclusively to describe equine height. 15.1 1/2 hands equates to 15 hands, 1 1/2 inches, or 61 1/2 inches at the withers.

[52] Peters, "Hyperion."

[53] Peters, "Hyperion."

[54] Yo Tambien, "Your Host–the Magnificent Cripple," 1998, <http://horseracing.about.com/library/blyourhost.htm> p. 1.

[55] *A Second Quarter Century of American Racing and Breeding, 1941 Through 1965* (Lexington, Ky.: Thoroughbred Owners and Breeders Association, The Blood-Horse, 1967), p. 284.

[56] *A Second Quarter Century of American Racing and Breeding, 1941 Through 1965*, p. 285.

[57] Associated Press, "Your Host Wins Derby Prep," *New York Times*, April 22, 1950, p. 16, col. 4.

[58] Arthur Daly, "Watchful Waiting," Sports of the Times, *New York Times*, May 5, 1950, p. 28.

[59] Daly, "Watchful Waiting," p. 28.

[60] A video of this race, displaying Your Host's stride, is available at <http://www.kentuckyderby.com/2006/derby_history/derby_charts/years/1950.html#info>.

[61] James Roach, "Middleground Beats Hill Prince in Kentucky Derby," *New York Times*, May 7, 1950, p. 4, col. 2.

[62] Robertson, *The History of Thoroughbred Racing in America*, p. 434.

[63] Yo Tambien, "Your Host–the Magnificent Cripple," p. 2.

64 Pat Johnson and Walter D. Osborne, *A Horse Named Kelso* (New York: Funk & Wagnalls, 1970), p. 20. A biography for juvenile readers.

65 Your Host had fractured his right ulna, the bone below the shoulder, in four places below the joint.

66 As recorded by Yo Tambien, "Your Host–the Magnificent Cripple," p. 2.

67 David Alexander, *A Sound of Horses: The World of Racing from Eclipse to Kelso* (Indianapolis: Bobbs-Merrill, 1966), p. 264.

68 Johnson and Osborne, *A Horse Named Kelso*, p. 20.

69 Johnson and Osborne, *A Horse Named Kelso*, p. 21.

70 Betty Moore, "Mrs. duPont Discusses Horse of Quintennium, Better Known as Kelso," *The Story of Kelso* (Woodstock Farm, 1965), p. 73.

Chapter 2

1 Various reasons would later be cited, all potentially corrected by gelding: size, weight, behavior, a faulty stride caused by interference with male parts, even the need to conserve pasture space on the small farm, allowing colts and fillies to graze together. Gelding did little to improve Kelso's weight or temperament, but it undoubtedly corrected any flaw there may have been in his long fluid stride. Years later when questioned, Dr. Lee would respond with confidence, "The results obtained speak for themselves."

2 The stifle connects the femur (housed in the rump) and tibia. Despite placement on the upper rear leg, the stifle is the quadruped equivalent of the human knee.

3 Pat Johnson and Walter D. Osborne, *A Horse Named Kelso* (New York: Funk & Wagnalls, 1970), p. 35.

4 Steve Haskin, *Kelso*, Thoroughbred Legends No. 21 (Lexington, Ky.: Eclipse Press, 2003), p. 32.

5 Phone conversation with Carl Hanford, November 14, 2006.

6 Interview with Carl Hanford, November 8, 2003, Wilmington, Delaware.

7 Phone conversation with Carl Hanford, September 30, 2006.

8 Phone conversation with Carl Hanford, September 30, 2006.

9 Phone conversation with Carl Hanford, September 30, 2006.

10 Steve Haskin, *Kelso*, 22.

11 Interview with Carl Hanford, November 8, 2003, Wilmington, Delaware.

12 David Alexander, "The Post Parade," *The Thoroughbred Record*, July 17, 1965, p. 250.

13 "Tharp Home First on Aqueduct Turf," *New York Times*, July 17, 1960, p. S-4.

[14] This is a bit of an exaggeration, as the first clocking doesn't appear until 1785, when Sloven won four-mile heats in 9:07, 9:09, and 8:47 at the old Maiden Head Course on Bowery Lane. William H. P. Robertson, *The History of Thoroughbred Racing in America* (Englewood Cliffs, N.J.: Prentice-Hall, 1964), p. 32.

[15] Joe Hirsch, "Kelso," *The Blood-Horse Golden Anniversary Edition* (Lexington, Ky.: Thoroughbred Owners & Breeders Association, 1967), p. 94.

[16] Interview with Carl Hanford, November 8, 2003, Wilmington, Delaware.

[17] "Kelso Takes $56,800 Race in Jersey," *New York Times*, August 4, 1960, p. 20.

[18] Interview with Carl Hanford, November 7-8, 2003, Wilmington, Delaware.

[19] Hirsch, *The Blood-Horse Golden Anniversary Edition*, p. 94.

[20] Pat O'Brien, "Berlo and Kelso Move into High Gear for Conclusive Late-Season Engagements," *The Blood-Horse*, October 8, 1960, p. 876.

[21] William R. Conklin, "Kelso's Record Clocking Captures Discovery," *New York Times*, September 14, 1960, p. 48.

[22] Interview with Carl Hanford, November 7-8, 2003.

[23] O'Brien, "Berlo and Kelso Move into High Gear," p. 876.

[24] O'Brien, "Berlo and Kelso Move into High Gear," p. 876.

[25] David Alexander, "Upset in the Mud," *The Blood-Horse*, October 13, 1962, p. 875.

[26] William R. Conklin, "Kelso Equals 40-Year Old Mark at Belmont Park," *New York Times*, September 29, 1960, p. 44.

[27] To that time, only Gallant Man had run a faster Belmont Stakes, in the 1956 rendition.

[28] O'Brien, "Berlo and Kelso Move into High Gear," pp. 876-878.

[29] "New York Report," *The Thoroughbred Record*, October 8, 1960, p. 38.

[30] Joe Agrella, *The Blood-Horse*, October 22, 1960, p. 1006.

[31] Agrella, *The Blood-Horse*, October 22, 1960, p. 1006.

[32] Associated Press, "11-5 Choice Takes $144,150 Gold Cup," *New York Times*, October 16, 1960, p. S-4.

[33] Bill Surface, "Hawthorne Wrap-Up," *The Thoroughbred Record*, October 22, 1960, p. 21.

[34] Robertson, *The History of Thoroughbred Racing*, p. 34.

[35] Robertson, *The History of Thoroughbred Racing*, p. 87.

[36] Robertson, *The History of Thoroughbred Racing*, p. 87.

[37] Robertson, *The History of Thoroughbred Racing*, p. 87.

[38] Robertson, *The History of Thoroughbred Racing*, p. 245.

[39] In 1990, following initiation of the Breeder's Cup Classic in 1984, the Gold Cup was reduced again, to one and a quarter miles.

40 Charles Hatton, *The American Racing Manual, 1961 Edition* (Chicago: Daily Racing Form, 1961), p. 67.

41 William R. Conklin, "Favorite Sets U.S. Record For Two-Miles in Gold Cup," *New York Times*, October 30, 1960, p. S-1.

42 Conklin, "Favorite Sets U.S. Record For Two-Miles in Gold Cup," p. S-4.

43 Mike Casale, "The 42nd Running of the Jockey Gold Cup," New York Report, *The Thoroughbred Record*, November 5, 1960, p. 12.

44 Hatton, *The American Racing Manual, 1961 Edition*, p. 92.

Chapter 3

1 To Delp's credit, Spectacular Bid proved himself a "great horse" indeed, racing through the age of four, winning twenty-six of thirty contests, and placing in three others. In 1982, he was elected to racing's Hall of Fame.

2 R.P., "Affirmed," Thoroughbred Champions, Top 100 Racehorses of the 20th Century, p. 54.

3 Charles Hatton, *Kelso*, p. 6. Small booklet provided to me by Carl Hanford.

4 William H. P. Robertson, The History of Thoroughbred Racing in America (Englewood Cliffs, N.J.: Prentice-Hall, 1964), p. 91.

5 Robertson, The History of Thoroughbred Racing in America, p. 91.

6 Robertson, The History of Thoroughbred Racing in America, p. 91.

7 Robertson, The History of Thoroughbred Racing in America, p. 92.

8 Hatton, *Kelso*, p. 5.

9 "From Lengths to Kilos," *www.sporting post.co.za/pages//ability*, p. 1.

10 "From Lengths to Kilos," p. 1.

11 "From Lengths to Kilos," p. 1.

12 Interview with Carl Hanford, November 8, 2003. Though no written record exists of this, Carl Hanford remembers, "he didn't weigh 900 pounds" as a three-year-old. The weight of 850-870 pounds is based on recall.

13 David Alexander, *A Sound of Horses: The World of Racing from Eclipse to Kelso* (Indianapolis: Bobbs-Merrill, 1966), p. 266.

14 This is a principle understood by backpackers. The backpacker who weighs twice as much as his equally fit companion can carry twice the amount of added weight with the same amount of effort.

15 Curiously, in colonial times, weight was adjusted for height, in addition to today's criteria of age, gender, and ability (William H. P. Robertson, *The History of Thoroughbred Racing in America*, p. 9).

16 Robertson, *The History of Thoroughbred Racing in America*, p. 502.

17 Charles Hatton, "Few Worlds Left for 'King Kelso' to Conquer," *Kelso*, p. 5.

[18] Walter Farley, *Man o' War* (New York: Random House, 1962), pp. 251-252.

[19] Bill Rone, "Kelso Ready to Go Again, Careless John Eyes Phoenix," *The Blood-Horse*, March 18, 1961, p. 603.

[20] Your Host's grave was later moved to Woodstock Farm. Today, he lies beside Kelso.

Chapter 4

[1] William R. Conklin, "Carry Back Favored to Defeat Eight Rivals in Preakness," *New York Times*, May 20, 1961.

[2] *Time*, November 10, 1961, p. 64.

[3] Joseph C. Nichols, "Our Hope Placed Second to Kelso," *New York Times*, June 18, 1961, Section 5, p. 4.

[4] Mike Casale, *The Thoroughbred Record*, June 24, 1961, p. 17.

[5] Casale, *The Thoroughbred Record*, June 24, 1961, p. 17.

[6] Bob Horwood, "'61 New York Sport Superb . . . And Kelso Even Better," *Morning Telegraph*, January 22, 1962, p. 13.

[7] Horwood, "'61 New York Sport Superb," p. 13.

[8] Joseph C. Nichols, "Kelso Takes Metropolitan Before 65,569 at Aqueduct," *New York Times*, May 31, 1961.

[9] Interview with Carl Hanford, November 8, 2003, Wilmington, Delaware.

[10] Mike Casale, *The Thoroughbred Record*, June 24, 1961, p. 17.

[11] Phone interview with Carl Hanford, July 30, 2005.

[12] Casale, *The Thoroughbred Record*, June 24, 1961, p. 17.

[13] Whisk Broom II spent most of his career in England. He returned to the States at the age of six. The Metropolitan, Suburban, and Brooklyn were his only races in this country.

[14] In 1913, the order of the Brooklyn and Suburban were reversed, making the Suburban the third and final leg.

[15] Mike Casale, *The Thoroughbred Record*, July 15, 1961, p. 27.

[16] Casale, *The Thoroughbred Record*, July 15, 1961, p. 27.

[17] Interview with Carl Hanford, November 8, 2003.

[18] Lou DeFichy, "How Good Is Kelso? The Best There Is," *The Blood-Horse*, July 15, 1961, p. 167.

[19] DeFichy, "How Good Is Kelso? The Best There Is," p. 167.

[20] Casale, *The Thoroughbred Record*, July 15, 1961, p. 27.

[21] Steve Haskin, *Kelso* (Lexington, Ky.: Eclipse Press, 2003), p. 86.

[22] Joseph C. Nichols, *New York Times*, July 23, 1961, Section 5, col. 1.

23 Phone conversation with Tom Trotter, November 21, 2006.

24 As with distance, there is a relationship between weight and time. Theoretically, two additional pounds add one-fifth of a second to time. By this formula, under standard "scale weight" of 126 pounds for a four-year-old, Kelso would have run the Brooklyn in 2:00 3/5, three-fifths of a second under the track record. By the same measure, Kelso would have equaled the track mark in the Suburban – despite his easy victory.

25 Robertson, *The History of Thoroughbred Racing in America*, p. 551.

26 Teddy Cox, "Kelso Smashing Brooklyn Victor," *Morning Telegraph*, July 24, 1961, p. 26, col. 3.

27 Lou DeFichy, "Kelso's Limit: 136," *The Blood-Horse*, July 29, 1961, p. 364.

28 Casale, "He's a Champion," p. 27.

29 M. R. Werner, "Horse of the Year–Again," *Sports Illustrated*, July 31, 1961, p. 46.

30 Hatton, *Kelso*, pp. 5-6.

31 Charles Hatton, "Mrs. duPont Exemplifies Racing's Sporting Spirit," *Morning Telegraph*, August 9, 1961, p. 1, col. 7.

32 Bob Horwood, "Kelso in Good Hands-Hanford, Arcaro," *Morning Telegraph*, August 10, 1961, p. 26, col. 5.

33 Robertson, *The History of Thoroughbred Racing in America*, p. 552.

34 Official racing chart for the September 4, 1961, Washington Park Handicap.

35 Associated Press, "Chief of Chiefs Takes Washington Park," *New York Times*, September 5, 1961, p. 46.

36 Associated Press, "Chief of Chiefs Takes Washington Park," p. 46.

37 David Alexander, "Old Shoes and Chocolate Sundaes," in *A Sound of Horses: The World of Racing from Eclipse to Kelso* (Indianapolis: Bobbs-Merrill, 1966), p. 270.

38 Whitney Tower, "The Best Race Horse in the World," *Sports Illustrated*, October 9, 1961, p. 18.

39 Mike Casale, "He Looked Great," *The Thoroughbred Record*, October 7, 1961, p. 12.

40 Joe Hirsch quoting Eddie Arcaro, "Runs Mile, Quarter in 2.00 to File Claim to Second Horse of the Year Title," *Morning Telegraph*, October 2, 1961, p. 1, cols. 7-8.

41 Casale, "He Looked Great," p. 12.

42 Whitney Tower, "The Best Racehorse in the World," *Sports Illustrated*, October 9, 1961, p. 19.

43 Tower, "The Best Racehorse in the World," p. 19.

[44] Tower, "The Best Racehorse in the World," p. 19.

[45] Charles Hatton, "Review of 1961 Races," *The American Racing Manual 1962 Edition* (Chicago: Daily Racing Form, 1962), p. 37.

[46] Joe E. Palmer, *The Blood-Horse Silver Anniversary Edition*, p. 131.

[47] Palmer, *The Blood-Horse Silver Anniversary Edition*, pp. 131-132.

[48] Palmer, *The Blood-Horse Silver Anniversary Edition*, p. 136.

[49] Mike Casale, "Tribute to a Champion," *The Thoroughbred Record*, October 28, 1961, p. 12.

[50] Hatton, "Review of 1961 Races," p. 37.

[51] Casale, "Tribute to a Champion," p. 36.

[52] Casale, "Tribute to a Champion," p. 36.

[53] Casale, "Tribute to a Champion," p. 12.

[54] Lou DeFichy, "And Still Champion," *The Blood-Horse*, October 28, 1961.

[55] This is an exaggeration. The official margin of Count Fleet's victory was twenty-five lengths.

[56] Hatton, "Review of 1961 Races," p. 38.

[57] As a gelding, Kelso was ineligible for the French event at Longchamp.

[58] According to David Alexander, 99.4 percent of American races at that time were contested on a dirt track (*The Thoroughbred Record*, October 31, 1964, p. 1479).

[59] Technically, the proper name for grass is "turf," not to be confused with the generic use of the term that refers to the sport. Grass or "turf" courses are normally located inside the main dirt track, making the oval and straightaways shorter and the turns tighter.

[60] *Sports Illustrated*, November 6, 1961.

[61] Joe B. Hickey, Jr., "Kelso Encountered a Tiger," *The Blood-Horse*, November 18, 1961, p. 1263.

[62] Hickey, "Kelso Encountered a Tiger," p. 1263.

[63] Bob Horwood, "Kelso Again Is Acclaimed," *Morning Telegraph*, November 26, 1962, p. 10.

[64] Interview with Carl Hanford, March 13-14, 2004.

[65] Alexander, *A Sound of Horses*, p. 277.

[66] Joseph C. Nichols, "T.V. Lark Beats Kelso," *New York Times*, November 13, 1961, section 5, p. 9.

[67] Though midway up the rear leg, the hock of a quadruped corresponds to the human ankle.

[68] Interview with Carl Hanford, November 8, 2003, 2004. Sail Cheoil was reportedly displaying signs of estrus.

[69] "Along the Racing Fronts: Kelso Sidelined Rest of 1961," *The Thoroughbred Record*, November 18, 1961, p. 28.

[70] Robert J. Clements, "Washington D.C. International," *The Thoroughbred Record*, November 18, 1961, p. 12.

[71] Charles Hatton, "Profiles of Best Horses – Kelso," *The American Racing Manual, 1962 Edition* (Chicago: Daily Racing Form, 1962), p. 89.

[72] Hatton, *Kelso*, p. 9.

Chapter 5

[1] David Alexander, "Lightly Rests the Crown," *The Blood-Horse*, May 26, 1962, p. 1058.

[2] Charles Hatton, "Champion's Head 'Model of Quality,'" *Morning Telegraph*, Thursday, August 10, 1961, p. 26, col. 1. As reprinted from "Profiles of Best Horses," *American Racing Manual, 1961 Edition* (Chicago: Daily Racing Form, 1962).

[3] Hatton, "Champion's Head 'Model of Quality,'" p. 26, col. 1.

[4] Hatton, "Champion's Head 'Model of Quality,'" p. 26, col. 1.

[5] Alexander, "Lightly Rests the Crown," p. 1058.

[6] Barney Nagler, Hanford and Kelso Brighten Stable on Gray, Rainy Day," *Morning Telegraph*, June 13, 1962.

[7] Teddy Cox, "Kelso Tops $111,900 Metropolitan Handicap," *Morning Telegraph*, May 30, 1962.

[8] Official racing chart.

[9] Joseph C. Nichols, "Carry Back Ties Aqueduct Mark in Winning Metropolitan," *New York Times*, May 31, 1962, p. 32.

[10] Nichols, "Carry Back Ties Aqueduct Mark in Winning Metropolitan," p. 32.

[11] Mike Casale, "New York Report," *The Thoroughbred Record*, June 9, 1962, p. 37.

[12] Official racing chart.

[13] Nichols, *New York Times*, June 17, 1962, p. 8.

[14] Continuing past the finish line to achieve a longer workout under race conditions.

[15] Nichols, *New York Times*, June 17, 1962, p. 8.

[16] *New York Times*, July 5, 1962, p. 32.

[17] Mike Casale, "He Was Rated by His Jockey," *The Thoroughbred Record*, July 14, 1962, pp. 31-70.

[18] Casale, "He Was Rated by His Jockey," p. 70.

[19] Bob Horwood, "Kelso in Good Hands—Hanford, Arcaro," *Morning Telegraph*, August 10, 1961, p. 7.

[20] "Kelso's Still in the Middle," *The Thoroughbred Record*, July 21, 1962, p. 37.

[21] *New York Times*, July 15, 1962, p. S-1.

[22] "Kelso's Still in the Middle," p. 36.

[23] William H. P. Robertson, *The History of Thoroughbred Racing in America* (Englewood Cliffs., N.J.: Prentice-Hall, 1964), p. 558.

[24] Steve Haskin, *Kelso*, Thoroughbred Legends No. 21 (Lexington Ky.: Eclipse Press, 2003), p. 112.

[25] Lou DeFichy, "Valenzuela Prefers Money to Championships," *The Blood-Horse*, November 3, 1964, p. 1130.

[26] Official racing chart.

[27] Pat Johnson and Walter D. Osborne, quoting an article in the *Morning Telegraph* (September 20, 1962), in *A Horse Named Kelso* (New York: Funk & Wagnalls, 1970), p. 68.

[28] Art Grace, "Training a Champion," *The Blood-Horse*, March 14, 1964, p. 580.

[29] Associated Press, *New York Times*, September 9, 1962, section 5, p. 1.

[30] Art Grace quoting Carl Hanford, "Training a Champion," p. 580.

[31] Joseph C. Nichols, "Kelso Wins Stymie for His First Stakes of the Year," *New York Times*, September 20, 1962, p. 4.

[32] Nichols, "Kelso Wins Stymie for His First Stakes of the Year," p. 4.

[33] Nichols, "Kelso Wins Stymie for His First Stakes of the Year," p. 4.

[34] Charles Hatton, "Kelso, Back at Tops Again, Horse to Beat in Woodward," *Morning Telegraph*, September 21, 1962. Clipping provided by Carl Hanford.

[35] Hatton, "Kelso, Back at Tops Again, Horse to Beat in Woodward."

[36] David Alexander, "Kelly's Himself Again," *The Blood-Horse*, October 6, 1962, p. 817.

[37] Alexander, "Kelly's Himself Again," p. 817.

[38] Alexander, "Kelly's Himself Again," p. 817.

[39] Official racing chart.

[40] Alexander, "Kelly's Himself Again," p. 817.

[41] Charles Hatton, "Kelso Runs to Best Form As Leaves Begin to Turn," *Morning Telegraph*, October 2, 1962. Clipping provided by Carl Hanford.

[42] Joseph C. Nichols, "Kelso Takes Woodward," *New York Times*, September 30, 1962, p. 4.

[43] Lou DeFichy, "Kelso Is Back in Title Race," clipping provided by Carl Hanford.

[44] To that time, only Count Fleet, Citation, and Gallant Man had run the Belmont Stakes faster.

[45] Joseph C. Nichols, "Kelso Wins Belmont Gold Cup," *New York Times*, October 21, 1962, section 5, p.1.

[46] David Alexander, "Another Title in the Making for the Gold Cup Winner?" *The Blood-Horse*, October 27, 1962, p. 1003.

[47] Nichols, "Kelso Wins Belmont Gold Cup," p. 4.

[48] Interview with Carl Hanford, November 7-8, 2003.

[49] Charles Hatton, "Kelso Seeks to Retain Title Against Foes of Top Class," *Morning Telegraph*, October 27, 1962. Clipping provided by Carl Hanford.

[50] Interview with Carl Hanford, March 8, 2003.

[51] Official racing chart.

[52] Official racing chart.

[53] Official racing chart.

[54] Interview with Carl Hanford, November 8, 2003.

[55] Joseph C. Nichols, "Kelso Is Expected to Run in $125,000 International Today If Turf Is Dry," *New York Times*, November 12, 1962, p. 40.

[56] Nichols, "Kelso Is Expected to Run," p. 40.

[57] Joe Hirsch, "Kelso," *A Second Quarter Century of American Racing and Breeding 1941 Through 1965, The Blood-Horse Golden Anniversary Edition* (Lexington, Ky.: Thoroughbred Owners and Breeders Association, 1967), p. 92.

[58] Hirsch, "Kelso," p. 92.

[59] David Alexander, "New Millionaire," *The Blood-Horse*, December 8, 1962, p. 1403.

[60] Louis Effrat, "Kelso Takes $54,000 Race," *New York Times*, December 2, 1962, section 5, p. 6.

[61] Effrat, "Kelso Takes $54,000 Race," p. 1.

[62] Associated Press, *New York Times*, December 2, 1962, section 5, p. 1.

[63] Charles Hatton, "Profiles of Best Horses," *The American Racing Manual*, 1963 Edition (Chicago: Daily Racing Form, 1964), p. 126.

Chapter 6

[1] Charles Hatton, "Profiles of Best Horses," *The American Racing Manual*, 1964 Edition (Chicago: Daily Racing Form, 1964), p. 90.

[2] Kelso's stride was measured by Carl Hanford in a workout at 23' 11". At four, Charles Hatton reported his "extended stride" as 24' 2" in a small booklet provided by Carl Hanford (*Kelso*, p. 6).

[3] Hatton, "Profiles of Best Horses," p. 123.

[4] David Alexander, "The Post Parade," *The Thoroughbred Record*, July 17, 1965, p. 250.

[5] Russ Harris, "How the Mighty Have Fallen," *The Thoroughbred Record*, March 2, 1963, p. 15.

[6] Harris, "How the Mighty Have Fallen," p. 15.

[7] Jobie Arnold, "In the Winner's Circle," *The Thoroughbred Record*, March 2, 1963, p. 19.

[8] Arnold, "In the Winner's Circle," p. 19.

[9] Art Grace, "Hurting All the Way," *The Blood-Horse*, March 23, 1963, p. 551.

[10] Russ Harris, "Ho-Hum!" *The Thoroughbred Record*, March 23, 1963, p. 15.

[11] Jobie Arnold, "Circles," *The Thoroughbred Record*, March 23, 1963, p. 26.

[12] Arnold, "Circles," p. 26.

[13] R. J. Clark, "He Won Again Anyway," *The Thoroughbred Record*, March 30, 1963, p. 15.

[14] *The Morning Telegraph*, June 19, 1963, pp. 1, 6, col. 2.

[15] David Alexander, "The Post Parade," *The Thoroughbred Record*, July 11, 1964, p. 184.

[16] Alexander, "The Post Parade," *The Thoroughbred Record*, July 11, 1964, p. 184.

[17] Charles Hatton, *The Morning Telegraph*, July 5, 1963, p. 1, col. 8.

[18] A reference to his stride—part bucking, part jumping—as he fought Milo's hold. Mike Casale, "The Rich Get Richer," *The Thoroughbred Record*, July 13, 1963, p. 156.

[19] Hatton, *Morning Telegraph*, July 5, 1963, p. 3, col. 8.

[20] Hatton, *Morning Telegraph*, July 5, 1963, p. 1, col. 8.

[21] Hatton, *Morning Telegraph*, July 5, 1963, p. 1, col. 7.

[22] Casale, "The Rich Get Richer," p. 156.

[23] Mike Casale, "Perfect Casting," *The Thoroughbred Record*, August 10, 1963, p. 541.

[24] Casale, "Perfect Casting," p. 541.

[25] Casale, "Perfect Casting," p. 738.

[26] William H. Rudy, "Mighty Kelso, Magnet and Marvel," *The Blood-Horse*, September 7, 1963, p. 678.

[27] Mike Casale, "New York Report," *The Thoroughbred Record*, September 7, 1963, p. 738.

[28] David Alexander, "The Post Parade," *The Thoroughbred Record*, October 5, 1963, p. 1014.

[29] Alexander, "The Post Parade," *The Thoroughbred Record*, October 5, 1963, p. 1038.

[30] Mike Casale, "New York Report: Permanent Tenant," *The Thoroughbred Record*, October 5, 1963, p. 1036.

[31] Whitney Tower, "Two Ladies in Search of the World," *Sports Illustrated*, October 7, 1963, p. 26.

32 Tower, "Two Ladies in Search of the World," p. 27.

33 David Alexander, "The Post Parade," *The Thoroughbred Record*, October 5, 1963, p. 1014.

34 Casale, "Permanent Tenant," p. 1209.

35 Hatton, "Profiles of Best Horses," *The American Racing Manual, 1964 Edition*.

36 Phone conversation with Carl Hanford, March 3, 2005.

37 David Alexander, *A Sound of Horses: A History of Racing from Eclipse to Kelso* (Indianapolis: Bobbs-Merrill, 1966), p. 266.

38 Whitney Tower, "Move Over Man o' War," *Sports Illustrated*, November 1963, pp. 36-37.

39 "News of the Week," *The Blood-Horse*, November 2, 1963, p. 1207.

40 Joe B. Hickey, Jr., "Kelso Encountered a Tiger," *The Blood-Horse*, November 11, 1961, p. 1268.

41 Tower, "Move Over Man o' War," p. 38.

42 David Alexander, "The Post Parade," *The Thoroughbred Record*, November 2, 1963, p. 1338.

43 Robert Lipsyte, "Kelso Biting Hand That Feeds Him," *New York Times*, November 11, 1963, p. 44, col. 3.

44 Robert J. Clark, "The 12th Running of the Washington D.C. International," *The Thoroughbred Record*, November 16, 1963, p. 1531.

45 Larry Shropshire, "Mongo Grabs Global Glory," *The Blood-Horse*, November 16, 1963, p. 1411.

46 Marshall Smith, "The Ugly Iron Duckling Rides Again," *Life*, November 22, 1963, pp. 126-132.

47 David Alexander, "The Post Parade," *The Thoroughbred Record*, November 30, 1963, p. 1621.

Chapter 7

1 Charles Hatton, "Profiles of Best Horses," *The American Racing Manual 1964 Edition* (Chicago: Daily Racing Form, 1964).

2 Carl Hanford, as interviewed by Betty Moore, reprinted in *The Story of Kelso* (Maryland: Woodstock Farm, 1965), p. 16.

3 Art Grace, "Training a Champion," *The Blood-Horse*, March 14, 1964, p. 580.

4 Robert Herbert, "Kelso in Stunner," *The Blood-Horse*, May 30, 1964, p. 1127.

5 Herbert, "Kelso in Stunner," p. 1127.

6 David Alexander, *A Sound of Horses: The World of Racing from Eclipse to Kelso* (Indianapolis: Bobbs-Merrill, 1966), p. 281.

7 Interview with Carl Hanford, November 8, 2003, Wilmington, Delaware.

[8] Interview with Carl Hanford, November 8, 2003.

[9] David Alexander, "No Alibis, But Possible Explanations," *The Thoroughbred Record*, July 4, 1964, p. 17.

[10] Mike Casale, "Return of the Champion," *The Thoroughbred Record*, July 4, 1964, p. 16.

[11] Alexander, "No Alibis, But Possible Explanations," p. 17.

[12] Joe Nichols, *New York Times*, June 26, 1964, p. 20, col. 1.

[13] Casale, "Return of the Champion," p. 16.

[14] Alexander, *A Sound of Horses*, p. 282.

[15] William H. Rudy, "Class Reports," *The Blood-Horse*, July 11, 1964, p. 76.

[16] David Alexander, "The Post Parade," *The Thoroughbred Record*, July 11, 1964, p. 184.

[17] Alexander, "The Post Parade," *The Thoroughbred Record*, July 11, 1964, p. 184.

[18] Mike Casale, "New York Report," *The Thoroughbred Record*, July 11, 1964, p. 174.

[19] Alexander, "The Post Parade," *The Thoroughbred Record*, July 11, 1964, p. 186.

[20] Reaction reported by Alexander, "The Post Parade," *The Thoroughbred Record*, July 11, 1964, p. 186.

[21] Reaction reported by Alexander, "The Post Parade," *The Thoroughbred Record*, July 11, 1964, p. 186.

[22] Alexander, "The Post Parade," *The Thoroughbred Record*, July 11, 1964, p. 186.

[23] Alexander, "The Post Parade," *The Thoroughbred Record*, July 11, 1964, p. 186.

[24] Alexander, "The Post Parade," *The Thoroughbred Record*, July 11, 1964, p. 186.

[25] Alexander, "The Post Parade," *The Thoroughbred Record*, July 11, 1964, p. 186.

[26] William H. Rudy, "Summit Stumpers," *The Blood-Horse*, July 25, 1964, p. 292.

[27] David Alexander, "The Post Parade," *The Thoroughbred Record*, July 25, 1964, p. 410.

[28] David Alexander, "The Post Parade," *The Thoroughbred Record*, August 1, 1964, p. 470.

[29] Alexander, *A Sound of Horses*, p. 286.

[30] William H. Rudy, "Bullet in Brooklyn," *The Blood-Horse*, August 1, 1964, p. 353.

[31] David Alexander, "The Post Parade," *The Thoroughbred Record*, August 1, 1964, p. 471.

[32] Mike Casale, "By Ten Lengths This Time," *The Blood-Horse*, August 15, 1964, p. 658.

[33] David Alexander, "The Post Parade," *The Thoroughbred Record*, August 15, 1964, p. 651.

[34] Alexander, "The Post Parade," *The Thoroughbred Record*, August 15, 1964, p. 651.

[35] *New York Times*, August 28, 1964.

[36] *New York Times*, August 28, 1964.

[37] John I. Day, "The First Six Years," in *The Story of Kelso*, p. 89.

[38] Red Smith, "Only Human," as reprinted from *New York Herald Tribune*, September 8, 1964, in *The Story of Kelso* (March, 1965), p. 10.

[39] Smith, "Only Human," p. 10.

[40] David Alexander, "The Post Parade," *The Thoroughbred Record*, September 12, 1964, p. 916.

[41] Conversation reported by Alexander, "The Post Parade," *The Thoroughbred Record*, September 12, 1964, p. 916.

[42] Smith, "Only Human."

[43] Smith, "Only Human."

[44] Alexander, "The Post Parade," *The Thoroughbred Record*, September 12, 1964, p. 916.

[45] Alexander, "The Post Parade," *The Thoroughbred Record*, September 12, 1964, p. 916.

[46] Alexander, "The Post Parade," *The Thoroughbred Record*, September 12, 1964, p. 916.

[47] Alexander, "The Post Parade," *The Thoroughbred Record*, September 12, 1964, p. 916.

[48] Alexander, "The Post Parade," *The Thoroughbred Record*, September 12, 1964, p. 916.

[49] Alexander, "The Post Parade," *The Thoroughbred Record*, September 12, 1964, p. 916.

[50] From Alexander, *A Sound Of Horses*, p. 290: "were no longer propelled by legs, but were plummeted forward by the great engulfing wave of sound."

[51] Alexander, "The Post Parade," *The Thoroughbred Record*, September 12, 1964, p. 916.

[52] William H. Rudy, "Kelso, The Magnificent, Returns," *The Blood-Horse*, September 12, 1964, p. 767.

[53] Joe Nichols, "Kelso Beats Gun Bow in Stirring Stretch Run," *New York Times*, September 8, 1964, p. 38, col. 1.

[54] Jack Mann, "Kelso's Kingdom," *New York Herald Tribune*, December 20, 1964. Clipping provided by Carl Hanford.

[55] Jay Hovdey, "Gun Bow gave Kelso a run for the money," *DRF News Archives*, drf.com, October 19, 2001.

[56] Rudy, "Kelso, The Magnificent, Returns," p. 768.

[57] Mike Casale, "Age Will Be Served," *The Thoroughbred Record*, September 12, 1964, p. 908.

[58] Alexander, "The Post Parade," *The Thoroughbred Record*, September 12, 1964, p. 917.

[59] Description by Walter Blum, as provided by Jay Hovdey, "Kelso Gave Gun Bow a Run for the Money," *DRF News Archives*, drf.com, October 19, 2001.

[60] Alexander, *A Sound of Horses*, p. 291.

[61] Related by Carl Hanford in phone conversation, May 20, 2005.

[62] Mike Casale, "A Picture Race," *The Thoroughbred Record*, October 10, 1964, p. 1172.

[63] Allaire DuPont as told to Tom Seavers, "Greatest Sport's Legends," *ESPN Classics*.

[64] David Alexander, "The Post Parade," *The Thoroughbred Record*, November 28, 1964, p. 1790.

[65] William H. Rudy, "Million-Dollar Bargain," *The Blood-Horse*, October 10, 1964, p. 1012.

[66] Joe Nichols, *New York Times*, October 4, 1964, section 4, p. 4, col. 6.

[67] Jack Mann, "Kelso's Kingdom," *New York Herald Tribune*, December 20, 1964. Clipping.

[68] David Alexander, "The Post Parade," *The Thoroughbred Record*, October 10, 1964, p. 1184.

[69] William H. Rudy, "Enter: The King," *The Blood-Horse*, November 7, 1964, p. 1314.

[70] David Alexander, "The Post Parade," *The Thoroughbred Record*, November 7, 1964, p. 1581.

[71] Alexander, "The Post Parade," *The Thoroughbred Record*, November 7, 1964, p. 1581.

[72] Nichols, *New York Times*, October 4, 1964, section 4, p. 4, col. 2.

[73] Rudy, "Enter: The King," *The Blood-Horse*, November 7, 1964, pp. 1313-1314.

[74] Alexander, "The Post Parade," *The Thoroughbred Record*, November 7, 1964, p. 1580.

[75] Alexander, "The Post Parade," *The Thoroughbred Record*, November 7, 1964, p. 1580.

[76] Phone conversation with Tom Trotter April 14, 2004, to confirm claim of David Alexander in *A Sound of Horses*.

[77] David Alexander, "The Post Parade," *The Thoroughbred Record*, November 21, 1964, p. 1732.

78 Steve Cady, "Soviet Jock Says His Mount Rates With Kelso and Gun Bow," *New York Times*, November 11, 1964, p. 53.

79 Joe Nichols, "Kelso Gets No. 5 Post in International," *New York Times*, November 11, 1964.

80 Alexander, "The Post Parade," *The Thoroughbred Record*, November 21, 1964, p. 1733.

81 Alexander, "The Post Parade," *The Thoroughbred Record*, November 21, 1964, p. 1734.

82 Valenzuela's description as reported by Jack Mann, *New York Herald Tribune*, November 12, 1964.

83 Alexander, "The Post Parade," *The Thoroughbred Record*, November 21, 1964, p. 1734.

84 Alexander, "The Post Parade," *The Thoroughbred Record*, November 21, 1964, p. 1734.

85 Alexander, "The Post Parade," *The Thoroughbred Record*, November 21, 1964, p. 1734.

86 Alexander, "The Post Parade," *The Thoroughbred Record*, November 21, 1964, p. 1734.

87 Lawrence K. Shropshire, "Kelso Takes Gun Bow and Honors," *The Blood-Horse*, November 21, 1964, p. 1491.

88 Alexander, "The Post Parade," *The Thoroughbred Record*, November 21, 1964, p. 1734.

89 Alexander, "The Post Parade," *The Thoroughbred Record*, November 21, 1964, p. 1734.

90 In 1924, The Bastard ran the distance in 2:23 on the undulating course at Newmarket. The previous American turf record, held by Pardao, was 2:24 2/5, the previous dirt record by Going Abroad, 2:26 2/5.

91 Jack Mann, "Kelso Won't Rest on His Laurels," *New York Herald Tribune*, November 12, 1964.

92 Alexander, "The Post Parade," *The Thoroughbred Record*, November 21, 1964, p. 1734.

93 Francis Stann, *Washington Star*, November 12, 1964, as reprinted in *The Story of Kelso*, p. 20.

94 Tom Nickalls, *Sporting Life*, London, November 12, 1964, as reprinted in *The Story of Kelso*, p. 12.

95 Newspaper clipping provided by Carl Hanford.

96 Interview with Carl Hanford, November 8, 2004, Wilmington, Delaware.

97 David Alexander, "The Post Parade," *The Thoroughbred Record*, November 28, 1964, p. 1791.

[98] Kent Hollingsworth, "The Best Horses of 1964," *The Blood-Horse*, February 6, 1965, p. 9.

[99] Jack Mann, *New York Herald Tribune*, clipping provided by Carl Hanford. Last sentence also appears in Jack Mann, "A Champion for All Seasons," *Turf and Sport Digest*, December 1979, p. 26, quoting his own 1964 article, "The Champ," for *New York Herald Tribune*.

[100] Rudy, "Enter: The King," *The Blood-Horse*, November 7, 1964, p. 1313.

[101] Mann, "Kelso's Kingdom."

Chapter 8

[1] Bob Horwood, "Kelso Beats Gun Bow in International," *Morning Telegraph*, November 12, 1964, p. 24, col. 2.

[2] Jack Mann, "Kelso Won't Rest on His Laurels," *New York Herald Tribune*, November 12, 1964.

[3] Snowden Carter, "Kelso Relaxes on Bridle Paths in Cecil County," *The Maryland Horse*, December 1964, reprinted in *The Story of Kelso*, p. 22.

[4] Carter, "Kelso Relaxes on Bridle Paths in Cecil County," 22.

[5] Charles Hatton, "Profiles of Best Horses," *The American Racing Manual, 1965 Edition* (Chicago: Daily Racing Form, 1965), p. 102.

[6] John Steadman, "Kelso: The Horse That Became a Legend," *Maryland Living*, January 10, 1965. As reprinted in *The Story of Kelso*, p. 26.

[7] David Alexander, *A Sound of Horses: The World of Racing from Eclipse to Kelso* (Indianapolis: Bobbs-Merrill, 1966), p. 268.

[8] Steadman, "Kelso: The Horse That Became a Legend," p. 26.

[9] David Alexander, "The Post Parade," *The Thoroughbred Record*, July 17, 1965, p. 251.

[10] William N. Wallace, "Kelso Third in Jersey Dash in First Start Since Last Fall," *New York Times*, June 30, 1965, sports section.

[11] Alexander, "The Post Parade," *The Thoroughbred Record*, July 17, 1965, p. 250.

[12] Alexander, "The Post Parade," *The Thoroughbred Record*, July 17, 1965, p. 251.

[13] Alexander, "The Post Parade," *The Thoroughbred Record*, July 17, 1965, p. 251.

[14] Phone conversation with Carl Hanford, September 28, 2005.

[15] Associated Press, "Kelso Wins at Delaware," *New York Times*, July 10, 1965, p. S-5, col. 2.

[16] Alexander, "The Post Parade," *The Thoroughbred Record*, July 17, 1965, pp. 250-251.

[17] Phone conversation with Carl Hanford, May 20, 2005.

[18] William H. Rudy, "The Star Shines Again," *The Blood-Horse*, July 31, 1965, p. 1787.

19 David Alexander, "The Post Parade," *The Thoroughbred Record*, July 31, 1965, p. 476.

20 David Alexander, "The Post Parade," *The Thoroughbred Record*, August 14, 1965, p. 643.

21 Alexander, "The Post Parade," *The Thoroughbred Record*, August 14, 1965, p. 643.

22 Alexander, "The Post Parade," *The Thoroughbred Record*, August 14, 1965, p. 643.

23 Charles Hatton, "Kelso Wins the 1965 Whitney by a Nose," *drf.com/sar/2003/history.html*.

24 Steve Haskin, *Kelso*, Thoroughbred Legends No. 21 (Lexington, Ky.: Eclipse Press, 2003), p. 180.

25 Hatton, "Kelso Wins the 1965 Whitney by a Nose," p. 11.

26 David Alexander, "The Post Parade," *The Thoroughbred Record*, August 14, 1965, p. 644.

27 Mike Casale, "And On He Goes," *The Thoroughbred Record*, August 14, 1965, p. 634.

28 Hatton, "Kelso Wins the 1965 Whitney by a Nose," p. 18.

29 Landon Manning, Chapter 11, *Extra Sugar for Kelso*, p. 35.

30 Joe Hirsch, "Kelso," *The Blood-Horse, Golden Anniversary Edition: A Second Quarter Century of American Racing and Breeding, 1941 Through 1965* (Lexington, Ky.: Thoroughbred Owners and Breeders Association, 1967), p. 97.

31 Kent Hollingsworth, "Saratoga—Kelso and the Sales," *The Blood-Horse*, August 14, 1965, pp. 1935-36.

32 Casale, *The Thoroughbred Record*, August 14, 1965, p. 634.

33 Alexander, "The Post Parade," *The Thoroughbred Record*, August 14, 1965, p. 644.

34 In later years, they were joined by Buckpasser, Dr. Fager, and Forego. In 1976, Forego was assigned an all-time record of 140 pounds.

35 Jay Hovdey, "Gun Bow Gave Kelso a Run for the Money," *DRF News Archives*, drf.com.

36 Joe Nichols, "68,558 See Malicious Win Aqueduct Stakes by 3 Lengths, Kelso Finishes Fourth," *New York Times*, September 7, 1965, p. 49, col. 1.

37 Nichols, "68,558 See Malicious Win Aqueduct Stakes," p. 49, col. 2.

38 Mike Casale, "Sport of Every Kind," *The Thoroughbred Record*, October 2, 1965, p. 1091.

39 William H. Rudy, *The Blood-Horse*, September 11, 1965, p. 2211.

40 Hirsch, "Kelso," *The Blood-Horse, Golden Anniversary Edition*, p. 97.

[41] Casale, "Sport of Every Kind," p. 1091.

[42] Casale, "Sport of Every Kind," p. 1091.

[43] Phone conversation with Carl Hanford, May 20, 2005.

[44] David Alexander, "The Post Parade," *The Thoroughbred Record*, October 23, 1965, p. 1279.

[45] Alexander, "The Post Parade," *The Thoroughbred Record*, October 23, 1965, p. 1279, Quoting an interview with Burley Parke by TV commentator Winn Elliot.

[46] E.L.B., "Kelso," *The Great Ones* (Elmont, N.Y. : *The Blood-Horse*/Thoroughbred Owners and Breeders Association, 1970), p. 159.

[47] "What's Going on Here," *The Blood-Horse*, January 1, 1966, p. 11.

[48] Charles Hatton, "Profiles of Best Horses," *The American Racing Manual, 1966 Edition* (p. 53.

[49] Art Grace, "Donn Goes Without Kelso," *The Blood-Horse*, March 19, 1966, p. 220.

[50] Grace, "Donn Goes Without Kelso," p. 220.

[51] *New York Times*, March 3, 1966, p. 39, col. 1.

[52] *The Blood-Horse*, March 19, 1966, p. 718. No byline provided. Assumed to be Editor, Kent Hollingsworth.

[53] David Alexander, "The Post Parade," *The Thoroughbred Record*, March 19, 1966, p. 759.

[54] Art Grace, "Donn Goes Without Kelso," p. 221.

[55] *New York Times*, p. 40, col. 1.

[56] *The Blood-Horse*, March 19, 1966, p. 718. No byline provided. Assumed to be editor Kent Hollingsworth.

[57] Alexander, "The Post Parade," *The Thoroughbred Record*, March 19, 1966, pp. 759-760.

Chapter 9

[1] Jim Kitt, "Worth the Price," *TracStar News* @ tracstar.com/newsarchive/060901.html, June 9, 2001, p. 2.

[2] Harlan Abbey, "Show Horses–A New Career for Racing's Millionaire," *The Canadian Horse*, October-November 1967, pp. 24-25.

[3] David Alexander, *A Sound of Horses: The World of Racing from Eclipse to Kelso* (Indianapolis: Bobbs-Merrill, 1966) p. 261.

[4] Alexander, *A Sound of Horses*, pp. 299-300.

[5] Abbey, "Show Horses–A New Career for Racing's Millionaire," p. 24.

[6] Abbey, "Show Horses–A New Career for Racing's Millionaire," p. 25.

[7] Abbey, "Show Horses–A New Career for Racing's Millionaire," p. 24.

[8] This is a rare mistake. Kelso actually won 13 of 24 efforts under 130 pounds or more.

[9] William H. P. Robertson, *The History of Thoroughbred Racing in America* (Englewood Cliffs, N.J.: Prentice-Hall, 1964), p. 549.

[10] Joe Hirsch, "Kelso," *A Second Quarter-Century of American Racing and Breeding 1941 Through 1965* (Lexington, Ky.: Thoroughbred Owners and Breeders Association, 1967), p. 93.

[11] John Moylan, "Remembering Kelso," *The Backstretch*, October 1985, p. 23.

[12] Jack Ireland, "Kelso's Handlers Like Funny Cide," *News Journal*, June 6, 2003, as appeared in Sports News, *delawareonline.com*.

[13] "Five-Time Horse of the Year Kelso Dies at Woodstock," *The Maryland Horse*, November 1983, p. 67.

[14] *The Maryland Horse*, November 1983, p. 67.

[15] Franz Lidz, "Scorecard," *Sports Illustrated*, October 31, 1983, p. 17.

[16] Lidz, "Scorecard," *Sports Illustrated*, October 31, 1983, p. 17.

[17] "Bright Days Remembered," *The Blood-Horse*, October 29, 1983, p. 7723.

[18] Joe Hirsch, "Kelso Dies in Md. at 26," [*Daily Racing Form* or *The Morning Telegraph*], Tuesday, October 18, 1983. Clipping provided by Keeneland Library.

[19] "Racing Fans Cheer Kelso and Forego," *New York Times*, October 16, 1983, sports section, p. 6, col. 1.

[20] *New York Times*, October 16, 1983, sports section, p. 6, col. 2.

[21] "Five-Time Horse of the Year Kelso Dies at Woodstock," p. 67.

[22] Steven Crist, "Kelso Dies of Colic at 26," *New York Times*, October 18, 1983, p. B5, col. 5.

[23] Crist, "Kelso Dies of Colic at 26," p. B5, col. 5.

[24] Hirsch, "Kelso Dies in Md. at 26," p. 5.

[25] Hirsch, "Kelso Dies in Md. at 26," p. 1.

[26] Joe Hickey, "Kelso Went Out Like a Champion, So Weep Not," *Daily Racing Form*, October 24, 1983. Clipping provided by Carl Hanford.

[27] "Transitions," *Newsweek*, October 31, 1983, p. 90.

Epilogue

[1] Paige Howard, "A Woman of Substance, The Legacy of Allaire duPont," *Maryland Life*, January-February 2006, February 26, 2006, <http://www.maryland-life.com/article_janFeb2006.jsp>

[2] Excerpt from written copy of Hanford's speech, provided by Carl Hanford, October 27, 2006, and actual comments as reported in online article: National

Museum of Racing and Hall of Fame, "Hanford, Boland, Cougar II Inducted," August 10, 2006 <http://www.racingmuseum.org/news/nrm-news-view-story-detail.asp?varID=124>.

[3] Higgins, "Kelso Defined Era and Standard in Racing."

[4] William Leggett, "Kelso ruled when the Gold Cup made kings," *The Racing Times*, October 5, 1991. Clipping provided by Carl Hanford.

[5] "10 best racehorse of all time," *Guardian Unlimited, www.observer.guardian.co.uk/print/0,3858,4021603-103977,00.html*, p. 4.

[6] John Powers, "Horsepower to spare, *Boston Sunday Globe*, June 1, 2003, p. 1, col. 1, p. 12, col. 1.

[7] Steve Davidowitz, "Across the Board," *trackmaster.com/retail/sd0605.htm*, June 24, 2005, p. 2.

[8] Like Secretariat's Belmont, Kelso's American record is technically a world record for a dirt track, though in truth, few other nations race on this surface.

[9] Daily Racing Form press release, November 1, 2003, <http://www.drf.com/about/pr110103.html> December 26, 2006.

[10] Joe Hirsch, "Kelso: Sustained Brilliance," *Daily Racing Form*, Monday, June 21, 1993. Clipping provided by Carl Hanford, page unknown. On March 15, 2005, I spoke with Joe Hirsch:

> Author: "In 1993, a reader asked who you thought was the greatest horse of all time. You said, 'Kelso.' Do you still believe that?"
>
> Hirsch: "Kelso compared himself favorably to five generations of horses. His dominance over such a long period swayed me to write that. I wouldn't defend it with my life. I have a great respect for Secretariat and his Triple Crown, setting records in all three races. And I have a great respect for Citation (references his three-year-old season). I still think Kelso's feat as best horse in five generations was something special."
>
> Author: "When was he in his prime?"
>
> Hirsch: "From the end of his three-year old season . . ." (voice fades) "Kelso's race in the International—the one he won—was phenomenal. European writers were overwhelmed by his performance."
>
> Author: "Were you there?"
>
> Hirsch: "Of course I was." (Hirsch was there for a week before the race.)
>
> Author: "It's always been debated whether or not he was a good grass horse . . ."
>
> Hirsch (before I could finish): "He was a *great* grass horse. Of course he was a great grass horse. His race alone at Laurel was enough to stamp his credentials."
>
> Author: "But a lot of writers said it wasn't really grass, that it was rock hard from drought."

Hirsch: "Baloney! I say baloney. You'll always have critics—those who want to find something to criticize. It was a good grass course. You had the best European and American trainers running their horses. They wouldn't have run if it wasn't . . ."

Author: "How much did the track contribute to the time?"

Hirsch: "It always does. It was good time, and certainly the fast track was a contributing factor. But it wasn't ridiculously firm. Kelso was brilliant. The time was a reflection of that. (pause) Kelso was authentic. He was an authentic great horse."

Author: "Have you ever seen a horse that could have beaten him at two miles?"

Hirsch (following another long pause): "Not that I've seen. That was another thing that made him so great—his endurance . . ." (voice fades)

Our conversation was ending, but I will never forget Joe Hirsch's unsolicited parting words: "He was a super horse—the best of the best."

[11] Lou DeFichy, "How Good Is Kelso? The Best There Is," *The Blood-Horse*, July 15, 1961, p. 167.

[12] Bob Horwood, "Kelso in Good Hands-Hanford, Arcaro," *The Morning Telegraph*, August 10, 1961, p. 26, col. 5.

[13] Whitney Tower, "The Best Racehorse in the World," *Sports Illustrated*, October 9, 1961, p. 19.

[14] Mike Casale, "Tribute to a Champion," *The Thoroughbred Record*, October 28, 1961, p. 36.

[15] ESPN Thoroughbred Classics, "The Woodward Stakes," presented by the New York Track Association, 2002, hosted by Jack Whittaker (NTR Productions in association with ESPN). That would not be the last time Arcaro's words would be remembered. Chick Lang, racing veteran of seventy-nine years, and former manager of Pimlico, was a close friend of Arcaro and his wife. On March 15, 2005, he related the following to me by phone: "We'd sit around in the evening, have a few drinks, and talk about great horses he rode. One night he [Arcaro] was talking . . ."

Arcaro: "Let me tell you something, Chick. I can't say anything while Jimmy Jones (Citation's trainer) is alive. Anytime anyone ever asked me who was the greatest horse I ever rode, I had to say 'Citation.' If I hadn't, I'd get a call the next day from Jimmy. But I'm going to tell you right now that the best horse I ever rode was Kelso. Wasn't even close between the two horses. He did everything you could ask a horse to do. Didn't have to carry a racetrack around with him. Could run from anywhere—on the lead, from behind, inside, outside—didn't need a roadmap. You asked him to run, he'd run. He had it all. All he wanted to do was get on a racetrack and run."

Lang: "What about if they ran against each other?"

Arcaro: "Wouldn't have been close—Kelso would absolutely annihilate him!"

16 Joe Concha, "Best Thoroughbred of All-Time? Kelso," MSNBC.com, msnbc.msn.com/id/4974676/print/1/displaymode/1098/, May 17, 2004, pp. 2-3. Carl Hanford would agree with Campbell. On November 8, 2004, I posed this question Kelso's long-time trainer:

"Carl, if you had to run Kelso in his prime, against the best horses that ever lived in their prime, what distance would you have wanted that race to be?"

A devilish grin swept the trainer's youthful face, as he prepared to play his trump card:

"Two miles, he chuckled, two miles."

Appendix

1 Kent Hollingsworth, "Kelso Became the Measure of Excellence Sustained," *Thoroughbred Times*, March 13, 1993, p. 28.

2 Charles Hatton, "The Judge's Stand," *The Morning Telegraph*, October 20, 1962. Clipping provided by Carl Hanford.

3 William Higgins, "Kelso Defined Era and Standard in Racing," *The Saratogian*, clipping provided by National Museum of Racing or Carl Hanford.

4 "Pedigree for Kelso," *Del Mar Turf Club* at *dmtc.com*. Accessible from multiple sources.

5 Track, American, and/or world records for a dirt course.

6 This includes allowing for differences in the distance of the race. Kelso conceded an average 15.5 pounds in 9 races less than 1 1/4 miles; an average 19.75 pounds in 4 races at 1 1/4 miles.

7 Includes factoring differences in the distance of the races.

8 36% of Kelso's stake races, and 32% of his stake victories.

Index

Acknowledgements

No book is complete without thanking those who helped make it possible:

My trusted friend and ad hoc advisor, Bonnie Brown, assisted the project from start to finish with patience, faith, and skill; my lifelong friend and neighbor, Debbie Soifer, shared and understood my enthusiasm for Kelso, and my good friend, Peggy Deutsch, provided unrelenting encouragement, proofing, and laughter.

A thank you hardly seems adequate for the contributions of my family: My daughter Susan and son-in-law Joe for unconditional love and support; grandson Joshua for providing the light in my life; brother Richard for sharing my stories; and companion, Paku, for waiting patiently at my feet for the computer to shut down.

A thank you is owed to those who helped turn a wonderful journey into a book: My publisher, Bruce H. Franklin, for believing in Kelso's story, and believing in me; my copyeditor, Noreen O'Connor, for making a rough manuscript a completed work of words; historian Allan Carter of the National Museum of Racing, for four frigid days of magic (mine) and tedious assistance (his); Collections Manager Beth Sheffer of the National Museum of Racing, for generously displaying Kelso's five Gold Cups during the dead of winter; Phyllis Rogers of the Keeneland Library, for more research assistance than required in responding to inquiries; and Racing Secretary Tommy Trotter, who generously shared his knowledge, time, support—and respect for Kelso.

I especially wish to thank and acknowledge Kelso's trainer Carl Hanford, the childhood hero whose human reality far exceeded the larger-than-life image of youth.